T. E. BROWN

THOMAS EDWARD BROWN

A Memorial Volume

1830–1930

Published on behalf of
The Isle of Man Centenary Committee
AT THE UNIVERSITY PRESS
CAMBRIDGE
1930

CAMBRIDGE
UNIVERSITY PRESS

University Printing House, Cambridge CB2 8BS, United Kingdom

Cambridge University Press is part of the University of Cambridge.

It furthers the University's mission by disseminating knowledge in the pursuit of education, learning and research at the highest international levels of excellence.

www.cambridge.org
Information on this title: www.cambridge.org/9781107458765

© Cambridge University Press 1930

First published 1930
First paperback edition 2014

A catalogue record for this publication is available from the British Library

ISBN 978-1-107-45876-5 Paperback

CONTENTS

ILLUSTRATIONS

To Sing a Song...

To sing a song shall please my countrymen;
To unlock the treasures of the Island heart;
With loving feet to trace each hill and glen,
And find the ore that is not for the mart
Of commerce: this is all I ask,
No task,
But joy, God wot!
Wherewith 'the stranger' intermeddles not—

Who, if perchance
He lend his ear,
As caught by mere romance
Of nature, traversing
On viewless wing
All parallels of sect
And race and dialect,
Then shall he be to me most dear.

Natheless, for mine own people do I sing,
And use the old familiar speech:
Happy if I shall reach
Their inmost consciousness.
One thing
They will confess:
I never did them wrong,
And so accept the singer and the song.

T. E. B. 1881

PREFACE

by

SIR CLAUDE HILL, K.C.S.I., C.I.E.
LIEUTENANT-GOVERNOR OF THE ISLE OF MAN

It has been my singular good fortune to be Lieutenant-Governor of the Isle of Man just at the period when the hundredth anniversary of T. E. Brown's birth was impending. The circumstance has served to give me a very special insight into the pride and strength of the Manx national consciousness, and has afforded me the privilege of being associated with a movement which is destined, as we in this little Island believe, to bring Brown's poetry and genius more conspicuously to the notice of the English-speaking communities the world over, and thus to serve a very definite imperial purpose.

The task of a Committee which aims at the preparation of a memorial volume such as this is, in ordinary circumstances, a very formidable one; and when we first got together to consider and devise ways and means we experienced moments of tense apprehension. We had material, and we had many volunteer workers. That, however, we all felt, was insufficient. To serve the purpose we had in view we must secure the aid and guidance of an authority in letters who could speak to the world about Brown not only as a man but as an eminent literary critic. In the minds of all of us one name stood out like a beacon. Sir Arthur Quiller-Couch had not only been at Clifton when T. E. Brown was Vice-Principal there, but was among the first of living critics to bring Brown's writings and poems to the notice of the public. As long ago as 1893 'to open a new book of his' was, to Q, 'one of the most exciting literary events that can befall me in now my twenty-ninth year'. The only question in our minds was, Could we hope that he would come to our aid?

Well, we had the temerity to approach him, and, thanks to the most generous and sympathetic manner in which he heard our petition, we have been enabled to launch our memorial volume with the certainty that it will have a double appeal to the public. It not only contains, in the Memoir which constitutes the core of the book, a record of Brown, as a man, couched in language which, to use Q's own words, 'is written memorably in English'; it also embodies a critique of Brown as a poet by one who will be accepted as an authority on the subject. And, if for no other reason, I am glad to have the privilege of tendering to him on behalf of the Committee, and of the little nation it represents, our most grateful thanks for the loving care and labour he has so unstintedly given to the task he so generously undertook.

This volume, then, we hope and feel, goes out to the world not merely as the pious offering by the Manx folk to the memory of their own national poet, but in a shape which will enable it to take its place on the shelves of all English-speaking lovers of beautiful literature, of memorable prose and poetry. Thanks to Sir Arthur Quiller-Couch we shall have done more than celebrate worthily our centenary—we shall have done something to bring added joy and pleasure to readers throughout the world.

INTRODUCTION

by

RAMSEY B. MOORE

H.M. ATTORNEY-GENERAL, ISLE OF MAN

The birth of a poet is a major event in the history of a people; and when with poetic genius he develops an intense affection for his native land, and identifies himself and his work with its life and interests—the soul of a nation becomes vocal. The vital importance of the poet is expressed in the well-known phrase 'Let me make a nation's poetry, and I care not who makes its laws'.

With some such consciousness the Isle of Man approaches the hundredth anniversary of the birth of Thomas Edward Brown, which took place on May the 5th, 1830; and with a desire to place before the public (and particularly the thousands of people scattered over the whole face of the world who call Ellan Vannin 'home') a memorial of the Manx poet, this volume has been conceived and published.

Brown was the greatest lover the Isle of Man ever had. No rival claims, however strong, no disappointment, however intense, neither the pressure of work nor the passing of the years, could dim an affection born in his earliest childhood and fostered by the very circumstances which, for so long, kept him and his love apart. He steeped himself in the life, the habits, the language, the thoughts, the humours and the tragedies, the strength and the frailties of the Manx people; and when eventually his *magnum opus*—the *Fo'c's'le Yarns*—

was published, he dedicated them, almost offered as a sacrifice, to his 'Dear Countrymen' and hoped that there they
'might see as in a glass what they held dear',

> of ancient heritage—
> Of manners, speech, of humours, polity,
> The limited horizon of our stage—
> Old love, hope, fear;

and spite of the onward flow of time and alien influences
might find in them 'an anchor for their Keltic souls'.

Brown's eye was for the future rather than for the present.
In the charming introduction to the *Fo'c's'le Yarns* he
addresses his *spes altera* to the future Manx poet who would

> strike the lyre
> With Keltic force, with Keltic fire,
> With Keltic tears,

and he was content to be the well from which the genius-
to-be should draw his water.

In a letter addressed to his sister Margaret, written on
November the 25th, 1894, Brown, with reference to the
contemplated publication of one of his works, expresses
very clearly his forward look:

I know what the future will think of the present, how it will stand
affected to our generation. Depend upon it, the last word has not
been said. A book of that sort, utterly neglected at the time it was
published would lie as dead as...a chrysalis; but it would have its
day, wings would lie hidden in the brittle case, and the light of a
clearer air would be for it to pierce through and permeate.

And now a hundred years have passed since Brown was
born, and thirty-two years since he died, and we desire to
affirm in no uncertain word that Brown is the richest

possession of the Manx nation. He is the embodiment of
the national spirit of the Manx people; the bond that binds
his fellow-countrymen the world over; his poetry the altar
round which these Keltic souls have their national com-
munion. All that is best in us, all that is noblest, ay, and if
you will have it so, our shortcomings—but anyway, all that
is truly *us* is embodied in his work, and the soul of the Manx
nation finds itself in his poetry.

But Brown is more—much more—than a 'local poet of
a tiny island'. He is gaining increasingly his place in the
ranks of the poets of England, and every day brings fresh
evidence that he is coming into his own. In addition to his
dialect poetry Brown left a mass of poetry—lyrical, narrative, philosophic—in classical English, in which he expresses,
in his own wonderful and often unique way, the thoughts
and experiences which formed his life, and the profound
truths which those experiences forced out of his soul. So
personal are many of his poems that we have good reason to
doubt if they were written with any thought of publication,
and most of them only saw the light when the Collected
Edition of his poems was published by his friends after his
death. I have no qualification to offer an opinion on the
merit of Brown's English verse. I know how they touch and
appeal and influence me; but in this volume their worth is
judged by those who have the right to speak on that subject.
Suffice it to say that seventeen editions of Brown's poems
have been published, and some of his verse has appeared in
almost every anthology produced in England and America
for the last thirty years.

In addition to his poetry Brown stands before the public in the volumes of letters published in 1900, letters which are read and re-read by those fortunate enough to have a copy of the volumes.

On the approach of the centenary date, Sir Claude Hill, the Lieutenant-Governor of the Isle of Man, gathered around him a Committee of about twenty ladies and gentlemen with whom he consulted as to the celebration of this event. This volume is the result of the Committee's decision, and how fortunate the Committee has been in securing the interest and enthusiastic assistance of Sir Arthur Quiller-Couch, His Excellency has expressed in the preface. On behalf of the Committee I desire to add a few words of acknowledgment to the other subscribers to this book. These names appear in the table of contents, and it would be invidious to mention any one in particular.

Viewing Brown from many angles, and helped by many who enjoyed his close friendship, we have in the aggregate a record, indeed a picture, of the man as he was; how he impressed them with his personality and gained their affectionate regard and esteem.

I must, however, make one exception, and that at the special request of Q. We are indebted to Mr William Radcliffe, ex-president of the London Manx Society, for his labours in gathering together the greater part of the material from which the biographical memoir was written. The Manx Museum is rich in Browniana, and Mr Radcliffe spent much time there and elsewhere working up the facts of Brown's life. He has well earned our deepest gratitude for his industry, ability and enthusiasm. We have also to acknowledge our indebtedness to Messrs Macmillan and Co. and Messrs Constable, for permission to draw freely on the volumes of the poems and letters published by those firms. As an acknowledgment of a personal debt I must also refer to Sir Hall Caine, who, at my request, prepared his memoir at a time when ill-health made any effort difficult.

I would like to add one word as to the deeper purpose underlying this book. Little is required from us to establish the name of Brown with the lovers of English literature. The leaven is working there, and nothing can stop it. But we do most earnestly wish to help the Manx people to realise the man God gave them in Tom Brown. It is the tragedy of popularity that it takes such strange perverted forms. The Manx people have never really *studied* Brown— they have been content to pick out the humorous portions suitable for popular recitation, and to a large extent they only know Brown as a comedian. Brown was a humorist— a rollicking humorist—a subtle humorist; he could wallow in it, and he could be withal as refined as a French satirist. To know him as a humorist and nothing but a humorist is to know only the smallest fraction of Brown.

May we hope that a perusal of this book may lead many to read Brown for themselves and to have the exquisite joy of entering a promised land flowing with milk and honey? It is the hope and desire of the Committee, and of those who have contributed to this volume, that the fuller knowledge of Brown now made available to the public may enlarge the numbers and deepen the intensity of his admirers, and lead to widespread interest in Brown's poetry and letters—the study of which will so amply repay the readers.

MEMOIR

T. E. B.

He looked half-parson and half-skipper: a quaint,
    Beautiful blend, with blue eyes good to see
And old-world whiskers. You found him cynic, saint,
    Salt, humorist, Christian, poet; with a free
Far-glancing luminous utterance; and a heart
    Large as St Francis's: withal a brain
Stored with experience, letters, fancy, art,
    And scored with runes of human joy and pain.

Till six-and-sixty years he used his gift,
    His gift unparalleled, of laughter and tears,
And left the world a high-piled, golden drift
    Of verse: to grow more golden with the years,
      Till the Great Silence fallen upon his ways
      Breaks into song, and he that had Love hath Praise.

W. E. HENLEY

MEMOIR

He hath made every thing beautiful in his time: also he
hath set the world in their heart. ECCLESIASTES iii, 11

I

In the early part of the last century Douglas, in the Isle of Man, was
a town with a population of about 3000,[1] mainly distributed along
the southern end of the bay and more closely congregated around
the northern margin of the harbour. Although the dwellings, many
of them miserable cottages, were for the most part irregularly
scattered and seemed to have been dropped rather than built, there were
numerous elegant structures fringing the North Quay, abodes of
wealthy traders, or warehouses with underground passages and
capacious cellars in which imported and exported goods (legitimate
and smuggled) were temporarily stored. A few of the buildings
remain to this day.

Almost in the centre of this North Quay stood the market place,
then an open square where on Saturdays farmers' wives and daughters
from all parts of the Island sold butter, eggs, poultry and other
produce of the land, hard by the stalls of the fish dealers: and on
Saturday evenings, when the farmers came with their carts to fetch
home their women-folk, there would often be lively scenes, chiefly
due to the *jough* sold in the surrounding public-houses.

Forming one side of the market square stood the old Church of
St Matthew's, the site of which has been incorporated in the present
covered market. This, the oldest church in the town, had been built
in the early days of the famous Bishop Wilson: but ecclesiastically
Douglas belonged to the Parish of Kirk Braddan, and both St
Matthew's and the more modern church, St George's, came under
the surveillance of the Rural Vicar, so that it was found necessary

1 The Census of 1921 puts the population of Douglas at 20,326; of the whole
Island at 60,000 about.

to pass a special Act of Tynwald legalising the marriages which had been celebrated in these Chapels-of-ease. In the year 1830 the Chaplaincy of St Matthew's was held by the Rev. Robert Brown, who, by virtue of his office, was also Master of the Grammar School and occupied the Master's house in New Bond Street hard by. (This name merely perpetuates the memory of former bonded stores—in fact there were large cellars under the Schoolmaster's house, and their rent provided part of his salary.) Though not far removed from harbour or sea, the house was surrounded by a network of insanitary alleys, some of which have since disappeared.

In this house, which still exists, on May the 5th, 1830, was born THOMAS EDWARD BROWN, sixth child and fourth son of Chaplain Robert Brown and his wife Dorothy: and in old St Matthew's Church he was baptised by his own father (who also, and many of his ancestors, had been baptised there), his Christian names being derived from his godfathers—the Rev. Thomas Howard, Vicar of Braddan, and the Rev. Edward Craine, Vicar of Onchan. Thomas Edward was an infant in arms; but on the same occasion his brothers Hugh Stowell, Robert, William, and his sister Dora, who had all been privately baptised by their father, received godfathers and godmothers. Sixty-five years later Brown wrote his last verses to aid a fund raised for a new St Matthew's Church, and characteristically had to excuse himself in a letter penetrated with affection for the old plain edifice and its memories:

I was baptised there; almost all whom I loved and revered were associated with its history.... 'The only church in Douglas where the poor go'—I dare say that is literally true. But I believe it will continue to be so....I postulate the continuity....

In 1832, the boy being then two years old, his godfather the Rev. Thomas Howard, Vicar of Braddan, took over the charge of St George's, Douglas, and transferred the Rev. Robert Brown from St Matthew's to Braddan, where though nominally Curate he was virtually Vicar, to which position two years later he was inducted.

BRADDAN—OLD VICARAGE

BY J. E. DOUGLAS

The change to the pure air of the open country must have been fortunate for the children; since the narrow streets, defective water supply and insanitary condition of old Douglas made it a fruitful ground for disease; and when cholera reached the Island later in the year, large numbers of the inhabitants died.

Brown, in one of his later lectures, pictured his arrival in Braddan as a child of two. His mother, he said, had told him that when they came up from St Matthew's it was his father's friends, the Drurys at Union Mills, who assisted them in setting up the beds, and it was William Drury—'tall William', with head almost touching the ceiling—afterwards his father's successor as Vicar of Kirk Braddan, who tucked him up in bed the first night.

The new home stood near the present Braddan Vicarage, off the main road away to the left, and about a quarter of a mile up the hill from the parish church. It was just a low whitewashed house, with a parlour on the left, a kitchen on the right, and behind that a little back-kitchen, over which was the bedroom of the boys: upstairs a room occupied by their parents, then the study and one little room for the girls. Nine in family occupied the house at one time.

The house, with a roof that sloped as in the old inns, was fairly well sheltered by clusters of trees surrounding a garden laid out in squares of fruit and vegetables, and bordered by flowerbeds, the flowers being chiefly moss and cabbage roses, narcissus and wall-flowers. The scent of these remained with the poet (always passionately fond of flowers) all his life, and especially the scent of wallflowers commingled with that of the sea. To the east the view included a strip of sea, bounded by Douglas Head. Fields lay beyond the garden—the scene of the potato-picking and hay-carrying described in *Old John*.

The old Vicarage has been pulled down; but its site can still be traced by the position of the trees which stand to the west of the present Vicarage—a sycamore to the south-west, an ash to the south, an elm to the north.

I wonder if, in that far isle,
    Some child is growing up like me
When I was child: care-pricked, yet healed the while
    With balm of rock and sea. . . .

I wonder if to him the sycamore
    Is full of green and tender light;
If the gnarled ash stands stunted at the door,
    By salt sea-blast defrauded of its right;
If budding larches feed the hunger of his sight.

I wonder if to him the dewy globes
    Like mercury nestle in the caper leaf;
If, when the white narcissus dons its robes,
    It soothes his childish grief;
If silver plates the birch, gold nestles in the sheaf.[1]

On one of these, which overhung Tom's bedroom, his older brother had fixed to the topmost branch a figure of Jupiter carved in wood; and to the imaginative child there was something mysterious in the wooden god. In after years he recalled how it haunted his childhood as he lay in his little room hearing the mighty Jupiter thundering in the tempest. They never took that wooden deity down.

But before telling of the inmates of the Vicarage, and their family life, one must say something of their ancestry.

According to Brown himself, his great-grandfather hailed from Scotland, came to the Island, and there married a daughter of the Rev. John Cosnaham, Vicar of Kirk Braddan, a member of an old and honoured Manx family. They had a son Robert and a daughter Anne, both baptised in St Matthew's, Douglas.

Robert became a sea captain and married Jane Drumgold, who, though a native of Douglas, was of Irish extraction, and whose family name is still perpetuated in the thoroughfare 'Drumgold Street'. Captain Robert Brown died young, leaving an only son

---

1 *Braddan Vicarage.*

Robert, who was educated for the Manx Church, married Dorothy Thompson (whose father belonged to Scotland and mother to Cumberland) and became the father of ten children, our poet among them. From this it will be seen that T. E. B. had in his veins the blood of Manx, Scottish, Irish and English ancestry. He once said at a Burns dinner, 'As a Manxman I of course have three legs. With one foot I stand on England; I have another on Scotland and a third on Ireland. What have I left for the Isle of Man? My heart, gentlemen—my undivided heart for dear little Mona'.

To go back to the great-grandfather's daughter Anne.—She married Thomas Stowell of Ramsey, and bore to him a family of fifteen sons and one daughter. One of her sons was the celebrated Hugh Stowell, Rector of Ballaugh; another was the ancestor of Amelia Stowell, who became the wife of the poet. Hugh Stowell of Ballaugh often visited Braddan, and although he died when Tom was but six years old the child preserved lively recollections of these 'angelic' descents; the little brass-nailed trunk containing the old saint's things; the hallowed room devoted to his service; the exquisite neatness of the man. Into this sanctuary he would take the children; and while they sat on the old trunk would teach them hymns and prayers, giving them little books and praying over them. Children (Brown said) never shrank from that venerable figure. It was as natural for a child to go up and place its hand in that of Hugh Stowell as to run and play. They sang to him and the sweet old voice sang to them. They liked his face, they liked his voice, they liked the touch of his hand, they liked to feel his breath on their cheeks.

When Hugh Stowell died, he was succeeded at Ballaugh by Brown's godfather Thomas Howard, who had married a niece of Stowell's and was therefore connected with the Brown family by ties of marriage as well as of friendship. He, in his turn, often visited Braddan.

By this time Tom was learning the rudiments of arithmetic and book-keeping from the parish schoolmaster, John Creer, afterwards a seedsman in Douglas. To Latin, however, and to the English classics, he was introduced by his father, to whom some words must now be devoted.

Robert Brown, Vicar of Braddan, was no ordinary man. His upbringing had been hard, and had left him stern and undemonstrative, with peculiar ideas due to an Evangelical training and a Puritanical boyhood. Hugh Stowell Brown has described his father as 'somewhat morose and combative'. T. E. B. remembered him rather as a melancholy man. 'It wasn't that universal melancholy which haunted all nature. It was the intense melancholy that preyed on the mind and had its source in personal and spiritual experience.' He seldom praised his children. He disliked and suspected all strangers. His motto was 'Manxland for the Manx', yet he cared very little for Manx history. He had a decided Manx accent, yet his idioms were pure English. Neither had he any liking for Manx music or Manx literature—he scarcely believed in their existence. Although he had never been at a University, his habit of mind was that of a University scholar. He was so fastidious about composition that he would make his son read some fragment of an English classic to him before answering an ordinary invitation! Many could not understand how a man so conspicuous for Evangelical piety could attach so much importance to a question of style and manner. But his son was not one of them. 'To my father', he said, 'style was like the instinct of personal cleanliness.'

In spite of his rigid opinions and his reticence in showing affection, the Vicar had a most tender heart. He was something of a poet too, and a considerable musician. He sometimes played the organ in church, and was the composer of two well-known hymn tunes, 'Hatfield' and 'Kirk Braddan'. He had also published a volume of poems in 1826, besides some satires in the Byronic manner, one of which had brought him an appreciative letter from Wordsworth, with a set of the poet's six-volume edition and an autographed inscription. Of his character as a parish priest his son has left this description:

To think of a *Parſon* respecting men's vices even; not as vices, God forbid! but as parts of *them*, very likely all but inseparable from them; at any rate, *theirs*! Pitying with an eternal pity, but not exposing, not rebuking. My father would have considered he was 'taking a liberty' if he had confronted the sinner with his sin. Doubtless he carried this too far. But don't suppose for a moment that the 'weak brethren' thought he was conniving at their weakness. Not they: they saw the delicacy of his conduct. You don't think, do you, that these poor souls are incapable of appreciating delicacy? God only knows how far down into their depths of misery the sweetness of that delicacy descends....He loved sincerity, truth and modesty. It seemed as if he felt that, with these virtues, the others could not fail to be present.

These noble idiosyncrasies—together with the love of scholarship, poetry, music—echoed through the life of his son; who worshipped continuity.

The Brown family knew very little of the gentry of Kirk Braddan, who had few inclinations towards literature:[1] but that the neighbouring farmers appreciated their Vicar may be gathered from the following extract from a local newspaper of the time: 'An excellent cow was presented to this exemplary divine as a token of respect and esteem from a number of parishioners as a Christmas gift, 1836'.

Tom attended the village school at Port-e-Slee under the wing of his brother Hugh, who had an early inclination towards natural science and mechanics and at that time intended to be an engineer. There, in intervals of music and singing, Hugh built his first steam engine, to the admiration of his junior, who spent some of his spare time in carving under one of the school windows the apocryphal inscription: *Hanc Scholam aedificavit totavitque Thomas Brunes Miles*

---

[1] An exception was Thomas Ogden, Attorney-General of the Island, a neighbour living at Kirby and a great admirer of Robert Brown's literary gifts.

(This school was built and endowed by Sir Thomas Brown). The inscription has long since been erased; and in one of his Manx lectures Brown afterwards lamented that his one chance of a modest immortality had been so ruthlessly destroyed.

He was about four years old when his father's sight began to fail, and reading became painful. Hugh came to the rescue and was his father's reader until he left home to qualify himself for an engineer; afterwards Tom had to take his brother's place. The reading was chiefly in preparation for his father's sermons, and the procedure generally as follows: (1) solid commentaries and serious authors; (2) illustrations from history and the English classics, including poetry. The boy then wrote down the sermon at his father's dictation; who, after hearing it in its finished form, would practise delivering it in a beautiful emotional voice. Thomas never wrote down his father's Manx sermons. These were discussed with the parish schoolmaster on Saturday mornings, to secure accuracy, for Manx to the Vicar was an acquired language. The sermons would be largely based on ecclesiastical history of the partisan type: for the Vicar cordially hated what he held to be Romanising tendencies in the Church of England. An ardent Irish Protestant supplied the family regularly with copies of the *Record* and *Christian Observer*, which also the lad read aloud. He often listened, too, to debates between his father and William Gill, Vicar of Malew, who stood for the middle school of Anglican theology. 'It was a great treat to hear Mr Gill and my father stirred up to the fire of debate. What earnestness, what skill, what fence, what dignified courtesy, what a model for young intellectual athletes! We listened: we did not dare to applaud.' Tom assisted, too, in the writing of controversial articles for the Press from his father's dictation. Among these controversies was a notable one between the Vicar, signing himself 'Manx Presbyter', and the Rev. J. G. Cumming, the Vice-Principal of King William's College, which appeared in the columns of the *Manx Sun* between 1840 and 1846. 'It was with weapons forged upon a tremendous anvil and proved upon the polished armour of Mr Gill that my father rose to the height of this great argument, and great was his exultation whenever he had cornered Mr Cumming.'

Cards, of course, were excluded from the house, all games looked upon with indifference, and quarrellings sternly forbidden. Nevertheless Tom managed to put in two fights with Douglas boys, one with a butcher-boy whom he beat. In the second he took a licking. The child frequented Douglas Quay whenever he could, and no doubt picked up from the fishermen there much of the vernacular he uses with such ease in his Manx poems. His earliest visits were haunted by a double terror; of his father's wrath and of the apprehension of meeting a tall black figure with horns and tail and cloven hoofs, having heard a man say that whenever *he* went into Douglas market place he saw the Devil very busy there among the buyers and sellers.

The Vicar had strong views, too, on books suitable for his children's reading. He would not knowingly allow novels inside his house—even Sir Walter Scott's, though he admired Scott's poems. Tom, however, managed to smuggle in the Waverley Novels, one immediate result being that his brother Harry and he lined their bedroom with historical pictures painted by themselves. When the parents came to inspect this gallery, the mother expressed her pleasure, but the father made no remark whatever. Brown's love for Scott's novels endured to the end. Two years before his death we find him confessing his delight on re-reading *The Fortunes of Nigel*. Already, by some instinct, he was trying to express his childish ideas in poetry; but the utmost commendation he received from his father was, 'That will do, Sir', or 'Go on, Sir'.

After this description of the Vicar it may seem strange that Byron should have been his favourite poet—or strange until we remember Byron's immense vogue in his day. It was so, at any rate, and Tom was often called upon to read Byron to his father. One day the old man thought he would like the boys to read *Childe Harold*, and sent Tom to Douglas to procure a copy. The bookseller, not having one in stock, told him that he had a poem by the same author that would please the Vicar just as well, and persuaded him to take *Don Juan* instead. 'This evening, Sir—this evening—we'll commence *Don Juan*', and in the evening Tom was started upon the first canto. He had read about two pages when the Vicar commanded 'Stop, Sir!—that's mere doggerel'.

It may be worth recording that, in reading poetry, his father would not allow Tom to use the unstopped line. He had always to make a pause whether the author indicated one or not. Unstopped endings interfered with the even flow of metrical melody which soothed him; and in mature years Brown agreed that a delicately hinted stop, though not logically required, was advisable.

Brown's mother, as has been told, was of Scots extraction, though born in the Island: and her son would often say how much of the latent Scotsman in him rushed to the surface when he found himself in Scotland, or taking part in some Burns commemoration. She was a diligent reader all her life, especially of poetry. She had a keen wit too—a more daring and masculine wit, her son said, than is common in women—and strong practical commonsense. He described her as 'a great woman'; and of his affection for her, of his consciousness of all he owed to her and had inherited from her, of his self-denying efforts to help her, there is testimony of every kind. 'Not in vain am I her son', writes Brown to his sister, in his thirty-fourth year, 'I feel sure of that. And, believe me, this is no conceit: one can't help feeling what one feels: and if I do feel a strict and native companionship with the mountains of either world, I will not deny it, and I will claim it as inherited from her.' 'As he became older', says Mr Irwin, 'I at least noticed a growing likeness to her portrait.' Among the children born at Kirk Braddan was a sister Margaret, afterwards Mrs Williamson, to whom in later years Brown addressed many affectionate and brilliant letters.

According to this sister, he was a shy boy and timid, with a shyness that never quite left him; but none the less, being naturally companionable, he lived *by choice* in the very centre of the family, and could do his lessons sitting with them and joining in their talk. The older brother Hugh was by contrast full of daring and vigour. (But the later career of Hugh and his fame in the Baptist Ministry are another story.)

No account of these early days must omit mention of John McCulloch—'Old John'—the old Scotch manservant and general family factotum; dour, crabbed, Calvinistic, of the seed of the Covenanters, intensely devoted to 'the Maister'—of whose religion he partly disapproved—grimly indulgent to the children. He hailed from Galloway, and had displayed something more than his countrymen's tenacity in seeking south, since in obedience to that instinct he had reached England by racing the tide across the Solway:

> Old John, do you remember how you ran
> 　　　　Before the tide that choked the narrowing firth,
> When Cumbria took you ere you came to Man
> 　　　　From distant Galloway that saw your birth?
> 　　　　Methinks I hear you with athletic mirth
> Deride the baffled sleuth-hounds of the ocean,
> 　　　　As on you sped, not having where on earth
> 　　　　　　　　You were a notion.
>
> What joy was mine! what straining of the knees
> 　　　　To test the peril of that strenuous mile,
> To hear the clamour of the yelping seas!
> 　　　　And step for step to challenge you the while,
> 　　　　And see the sunshine of your constant smile!
> I loved you that you dared the splendid danger;
> 　　　　I loved you that you landed on our Isle
> 　　　　　　　　A helpless stranger.

It was John McCulloch who taught the children to dig, to carry the harvest, to know the ways and 'points' of beast and bird; and when the day was over the old man could be heard 'wrastling' with the Lord in his own little room above the stable, interceding (though 'not of our kin or of our Church') for the family, one after another by name; or again on Sundays trapesing up the hill to his whitewashed chapel after attending the 'red mosaic' of Church of England service at Matins or Evensong:

> ...Nor then you had enough;
> But, with your waistcoat-pocket full of snuff
> You scorned the flesh, suppressed the stomach's clamour,
> And went where you could get 'the rael stuff'
> Absolved from grammar.

Other friends and neighbours of childhood were James Corran, the parish clerk, with Mrs Corran, the saintly and absolute perfection of an old Manx farmer's wife; the washerwoman in the nearest cottage, a widow, and her numerous children. From these and from 'Old John' he unconsciously learnt his understanding of the poor, and his beautiful manners towards all sorts and conditions of men.

If we have seemed to dwell in too much detail upon the circumstances of his childhood the answer is found in the tenacity of Brown's home affections and his passionate lifelong regard for these early days and native scenes. Many of us—perhaps the most of us—drop into life, so to speak, as a stone into a pool, the effect of our incidence spreading itself in wider and wider circles. Brown's career, as will be seen, extended to no great distance and exhibits no great shock of incident, though his influence both as schoolmaster and poet has widened far since his death. But his emotions, especially toward the close, will be found to be quite curiously centripetal, narrowing down still more and more intensely upon his beloved Island. It is said that all children exploring for themselves and astray in their bearings have a natural tendency to walk up-hill, so that in searching for any lost child you will do wisely to make for the highest neighbouring point within the compass of his strength. Brown made this adventure at the age of eight, and was tremendously proud of his first climb. He felt a throb of surprise on discovering that the Island was so much larger than he had believed—that the south side was not everything. He saw the extent of the north side with a vision of its beauty, and longed to explore it.

In 1843, after some years of training as an engine-driver, his brother Hugh decided to enter the Ministry of the Church. His father demurred; for to him the Ministry had been a life of poverty and hardship. The mother however had always wanted Hugh to be a Minister, and in the end it was decided that Hugh should go to King William's College. He could not enter for several months, owing to a disastrous fire at the College, and therefore read Latin at home with his father.

In the following year (August, 1845) the Vicar had a serious nervous breakdown, but carried on his duties with assistance. Hugh now often walked home to Braddan and returned to Castletown the same evening. By this time his father had begun to look to him for help as his curate. The Bishop, however, wanted him to be a kind of teacher-parson at Foxdale and would not license him to the curacy. Moreover Hugh had begun to develop doubts on the doctrine of Baptism, and finally gave up the idea of ordination in the Church of England. He left home in August, 1846, and was invited to preach at Myrtle Street Baptist Chapel, Liverpool; chosen a few months afterwards as its Minister at the age of twenty-three; and thus opened a notable career. Troubles now began to thicken upon the household at the Vicarage. Tom had just been entered as a day boy at King William's College when Hugh left home. Within a few weeks the father had a serious relapse, and Hugh returned to find the household in great distress. He remained at home about a fortnight, greatly comforting all. But in October news arrived of the death of Robert (the eldest brother) in the Bahamas at the age of twenty-six; and, early in November, Harry, a younger brother, died at home. Once more Hugh returned to the Island, and on November the 28th set out from Kirk Braddan for Douglas in the middle of a great snowstorm, to catch the Liverpool boat.

A few hours afterwards John McCulloch found the father lying dead in the snow, not many yards from the Vicarage. He had gone out with the intention of overtaking Hugh and dissuading him from crossing in such a gale.

Robert Brown was buried in the south-west corner of the church-yard of Old Kirk Braddan.

II

At the time of his father's death T. E. B. was sixteen; his sister Margaret a girl of twelve. There were also a son William, serving his apprenticeship as a sailor; Alfred, a child of seven; and two daughters who died in early life but are said to have inherited their mother's wit and humour.

For the sake of a home close to the College Brown's mother removed the household early in 1847 to The Green at Castletown, her unmarried sister, Miss Thompson (who had a small private income) joining them. The mother and the children under age were entitled to certain diocesan grants, and Brown himself, as a clergy-man's son, to free education at King William's College.

The Principal of King William's College at that time was the Rev. Dr Dixon, a clergyman of Evangelical views; the Vice-Principal, the Rev. J. G. Cumming (already alluded to, p. 10), an authority on the geology of the Island.

The College at that time sheltered many pupils fated to win distinction in after-life. The head boy in Brown's first year was F. W. Farrar, afterwards famous as preacher, Headmaster of Marlborough, and author of *The Life of Christ*. He also wrote, among other popular tales, that mawkish but over-derided story of school life, *Eric, or Little by Little*, the school therein depicted being supposedly King William's College. Farrar died Dean of Canterbury. In 1847 all the school's principal prizes fell to him, including the first poetry prize, Brown not competing. Other friends of Brown's at school were E. S. Beesly (afterwards Professor), Thomas Fowler (afterwards Professor of Logic at Oxford, President of Corpus Christi College and Vice-Chancellor of the University);

and James Maurice Wilson. Wilson had a very brilliant academic career at St John's College, Cambridge, and was senior wrangler in 1859. He became successively assistant master at Rugby, Headmaster of Clifton, Archdeacon of Manchester, Canon of Worcester, and is still living (1930) aged ninety-four. Wilson was too much Brown's junior to be noticed by him at the school; but his recollections, coloured by a boy's hero-worship, are extremely vivid. Later life brought the two into close association; and this book is indebted to Canon Wilson for a chapter of reminiscences, printed as an appendix, to which the reader is referred for many details.

Fowler and Brown became close friends. 'As soon', records Fowler, 'as we began to have our lessons together, we seemed drawn to each other by some natural affinity. We were both day boys, and, as our roads lay in the same direction, frequently walked home or to school together. Our intimacy matured, and these casual walks were soon developed into afternoon walks on half-holidays. On these occasions our conversation was not about athletics, as it might have been in these days, but about literature, history, politics, theology, and, perhaps above all, about the beautiful scenery amidst which we rambled. To those who know the southern portion of the Isle of Man, the attraction of this last topic will not seem strange when I mention the rocks at Scarlett, South Barrule, Langness Point, Derby Haven, Ballasalla, Kirk Malew, Kirk Santon, etc. Brown was already an enthusiast about the scenery of his native Island, and it was not long after our acquaintance began before I detected the touch of genius which was characteristic of him throughout life.' We must mention another friend of Brown's schooldays—his cousin, H. S. Gill, son of the Vicar of Malew, who in course of time became Archdeacon of the Island when that honour had been offered to Brown and declined. Gill's early memories are of an 'emphatically and manly vigorous boy; but, being a day boy, he was seldom at school during play hours. He had a strong sense of humour and a keen eye for any peculiarity of voice, accent or manner. Sometimes his power of mimicry gave offence to those who did not know how incapable he was of willingly hurting people's feelings'. Brown's mimicry was really unconscious. He couldn't report a conversation between himself and another without acting both parts.

But the friend who, at the critical crossroads of life as Brown was leaving school, determined his future path was an older man— Archdeacon Moore, Rector of Andreas. Moore had known him from infancy, and now, greatly impressed by the boy's brilliant compositions in Greek, Latin and English, strongly advised his going up to a University, and discussed with him the ways and means. Some friends had suggested Dublin, it being possible to stand for a degree there without residence. To those who have any sentiment about the University, and not least to all who have a sentiment about Trinity College, Dublin, this procedure will be understood as no less repugnant to most boys of eighteen than it was to Brown, whose object, he said, was 'not a Degree to cover my nakedness but the acquisition of academical learning'.

Some description of this beneficent man, Archdeacon Moore, may be given here, and can hardly be better indicated than in Brown's own account of a visit to Andreas Rectory:

It was on a very bright frosty night at Christmastide of 1848–1849 that I rode with him in his carriage from Tromode to Andreas. Our companion, besides Cannell, was Mr Trollope, at that time I think curate of Jurby. To see the Archdeacon at home was to learn to love him. The very arrangements of that home, its order, its simplicity, its decent regard of ancient usage, the spirit it breathed of peace and good-will, the affectionate devotion of servant to master and master to servant, the perfect concord—all this irresistibly attracted me to him who was the very key and centre of this harmony.

The Christmas dinner was a scene never to be forgotten. It was held in the large kitchen of the Rectory: all the servants of the household were of course there, besides all those who worked in any capacity on the glebe. The Archdeacon presided. In the midst of all the brightness and happiness a strange weird face was seen at the door, a face whose weakness was redeemed by a smile of heavenly quietude—it was an old friend of mine, a still older friend perhaps of the Archdeacon, Chalse-y-Killey. Chalse was heartily welcomed. There was nothing more remarkable in the Archdeacon than his unfeigned compassion for poor innocents. He seemed to look upon them as children, his own children, and yearn over them with a tenderness curiously blended with playfulness. I never have witnessed the mind of Christ so lively expressed in mortal face or voice.

This Chalse-y-Killey was a poor half-wit 'character' of the Island, garbed in many colours and wearing a top-hat battered to concertina shape: and his intrusion upon the company, with the Archdeacon's gentle welcome, must have cost Tom a twinge; remembering, as he must have, his own first meeting with the poor creature at Rushen Vicarage, when he and Parson Corrin's children had enticed the poor fellow to mount the pulpit and hold a mock missionary meeting. Later, he made ample and characteristic amends in a poem of which Chalse is the eponymous hero:

> Such music as you made, dear Chalse!
>   With that crazed instrument
> That God had given you here for use—
> You will not wonder now if it did loose
>   Our childish laughter, being writhen and bent
>   From native function—was it not, sweet saint?
> But when such music ceases,
> 'Tis God that takes to pieces
>   The inveterate complication
>   And makes a restoration,
> Most subtle in its sweetness,
> Most strong in its completeness,
> Most constant in its meetness;
>   And gives the absolute tone,
>   And so appoints your station
>   Before the throne—
>   Chalse, poor Chalse.[1]

[1] Brown always believed, in spite of eugenists and others, that half-wits, and even sinners, were sent into the world for our general good. A belief not

The discussion of ways and means ended in Brown's admission, through the Archdeacon's interest, to a 'servitorship' at Christ Church, Oxford; whither he proceeded in October, 1849, with a Barrow Exhibition, which carried with it a sort of moral obligation to render service to the Manx Church.

dissimilar from the above informs his poem on Catherine Kinrade—a poor sinful woman condemned in 1713 by the famous Bishop Wilson to be dragged through the sea after a boat for her offences. Brown pictures Wilson as standing before the Throne of Heaven, and being confronted there by a woman clothed in white seated on its step:

> Then, trembling, he essayed
> To speak—'Christ's mother, pity me!'
> Then answered she—
> 'Sir, I am Catherine Kinrade'.
>
> Even so—the poor dull brain,
>   Drenched in unhallowed fire,
> It had no vigour to restrain—
>   God's image trodden in the mire
> Of impious wrongs—whom last he saw
> Gazing with animal awe
> Before his harsh tribunal, proved unchaste,
> Incorrigible, woman's form defaced
> To uttermost ruin by no fault of hers—
> So gave her to the torturers.
>
> And now—some vital spring adjusted,
> Some faculty that rusted
> Cleansed to legitimate use—
> Some undeveloped action stirred, some juice
> Of God's distilling dropt into the core
> Of all her life—no more
> In that dark grave entombed,
> Her soul had bloomed...
> To perfect woman—woman made to honour,
> With all the glory of her youth upon her.
> And from her lips and from her eyes there flowed
>   A smile that lit all Heaven—the angels smiled;
> God smiled, if that were smile beneath the state that glowed
>   Soft purple—and a voice—'Be reconciled'....

III

The benefits—especially the ultimate benefits—Brown derived from
Oxford were inestimable; but they cost him almost intolerable pain.
The choice of his College had been imposed upon him by circumstances, but of all Colleges ChristChurch in the early 'fifties of the
last century was the cruellest nursing-mother for a poor but high-
spirited lad. It numbered many eminent sons, but was characteristically
the College of young aristocrats and sons of the rich, among whom
the position of servitor was not only by tradition but officially a
menial one.

He had expected some drawbacks; but when he found out the
reality he was filled at first with dismay, next with indignation, then
with smouldering disgust and hatred. No 'commoner' of Christ
Church would call on, or be seen speaking to, a servitor. The
servitors did not dine with the rest of the College, but nearly an
hour later, when they were served with the leavings of the other
tables, when they had frequently to witness flirtations between male
and female College servants and listen to rude laughter and bad
language; these servants being, as usually happens, more snobbish
than their masters. The Chapel of ChristChurch is the Cathedral,
and there the servitors were railed off from the rest. Their dress was
different. They could not be members of the Boating or the Cricket
Club—could not indeed be members of any club.

They were humiliated with a special gown with unpleated strings
and a cap without a tassel. To the rest of the College they were 'a set
of cads'. Men of other Colleges shunned them: their fellow-
collegians of 'the House'—*Ædes Christi*—never called on them:
neither tutor nor Chaplain (the latter usually an ex-servitor) would
invite them to a friendly meal. 'I had an old schoolfellow and most
intimate friend at [Ch.Ch.]. He was good, but not bold....I went
once or twice to his rooms, of course scrupulously servitorial in my

dress. I saw he did not like it.... I noticed his anxiety that I should come at appointed times; when I went he was always alone. Twice I think, but late at night, he came to my cellar in Canterbury Quad. Then, of course, the unnatural effort made me vehemently and morbidly suspicious. Why say more? Such relations cannot last.'

'It matters not', says Dr E. J. Martin, writing in *The Church Quarterly*, Oct. 1929, 'if other servitors did not see their position so darkly. This was how Brown saw it....' And in some measure it goes to explain (if one mistakes not) how he, the shy young Islander, so easily renounced Oxford and turned from it toward home, nursing the bite of humiliation, too quickly resentful of our whole confident, heedless English:

> Or, older grown, suspects a braggart race,
>   Ignores phlegmatic claim
> Of privileged assumption, holding base
>   Their technic skill and aim.

These and other humiliations were afterwards removed, partly by the intervention of the late Mr Gladstone (himself an old member of 'the House'), partly also in consequence of an article Brown himself contributed in 1868 to *Macmillan's Magazine*; 'And though', says Mr Irwin, 'I have heard that there is exaggeration in this article, there is no doubt he did not exaggerate what the position was to him. I have heard him refer to it over and over again with a dispassionate bitterness which there was no mistaking'. At the time, of course, he hid all this from his mother, and his letters home mainly record happy walks around Oxford in the intervals of reading twelve hours a day—a diligence rewarded by his election to a 'Boulter Scholarship', which eased his finances and enabled him to write home promptly that 'the greatest of earthly blessings is the ability to administer to the wants of those near and dear to me'. In May, 1851, again, he headed the list in his College examination, gained a further Exhibition, and was henceforth able to allow himself a little more physical recreation, his favourite exercises being rowing

and walking, with music always a great solace—as perhaps it was at all times the greatest solace of his life. 'R. possesses an excellent piano and was agreeably surprised to find that I was more than a match for him on that instrument. I do not know of anything that gave me more pleasure during the whole Term than that pleasant ramble over the keys after my two months' fast.' He was also allowed to browse in ChristChurch's magnificent library.

His strong point (it hardly needs saying) was Classics. For Mathematics he had little liking, even small respect,[1] but worked at these with the help of a friendly tutor. Eventually in 1853 he won his Double First (1) in 'Greats', and (2) in Law and Modern History.

Then the blow fell. His letters had been full of the kindness and appreciation of Dean Gaisford 'in all his dealings with me'. Yet that excellent man and famous scholar, for whom Brown had an unbounded admiration, absolutely refused to nominate him after his two First Classes to a Fellowship, though all the resident Dons desired it. '"A Servitor", he says, "never has been elected Student— *ergo* he never shall be"—an interesting specimen of ratiocination!!' Small wonder that the night after he won his Double First was 'one of the most intensely miserable I was ever called upon to endure'.

Relief and recompense, however, came to him in the following April with his election as Fellow of Oriel: for at that epoch, through the reflected glory of Newman, Clough, Matthew Arnold and others, an Oriel Fellowship carried with it a high and particular reputation.[2]

'This is none of your empty honours,' he wrote to his mother, 'it gives me an income of about £300 per annum as long as I choose

1 His friend Mozley on one occasion visited Brown in the Island and wrote: 'He took me to the top of the cliff near Port Erin, which overlooks a great obelisk of rock standing upright in the sea. I a little astonished him by attempting to measure the height of the cliff by dropping a stone into the sea from the top and timing the fall. Brown was not mathematical, and whether the cliff was 200 or 2000 feet high was to him perfectly indifferent'.

2 Among the examiners in 1854 were James Fraser and Benjamin Jowett, illustrious pair.

to reside at Oxford, and about £220 in cash if I reside elsewhere. In addition to this it puts me in a highly commanding position for pupils, so that on the whole I have every reason to expect that (except perhaps the first year) I shall make between £500 and £600 altogether per annum. So you see, my dear mother, that your prayers have not been unanswered, and that God will bless the generation of those who humbly strive to serve Him....I have not omitted to remark that the election took place on April 21st, the anniversary of your birth and marriage.'

The brilliant young scholar had at length the ball at his feet. Pupils came to him in plenty, and he could enjoy his vacations in walking tours about the Isle of Man and visits to his old friends Archdeacon Moore, Thomas Howard and William Drury in his new Vicarage at Braddan. Here he met that Keltic enthusiast Prince Lucien Bonaparte, who was learning the Manx language under the guidance of Drury and his mother.[1] The same summer he again met the Prince at Ballaugh Rectory, and next day at Jurby Vicarage, when the deference paid by the visitor to these Manx clerics was noted as charming. At Jurby, Prince Lucien took down the Lord's Prayer in Manx from the dictation of the Vicar, Mr Harrison; and afterwards, on a challenge to read back what he had written down, did so with a pronunciation hardly distinguishable from that of a native. After this they spent three hours discussing various subjects, including a dish of Manx porridge.[2] Another acquaintance made by Brown on these vacation rambles was Edward Forbes, the Manx naturalist.

But Oriel had sunk for a time—under the well-intentioned Provost Hawkins—from its high intellectual eminence. Its Fellows, the newly elected ones, were just plain, good, ordinary men. Nor did Brown (so far as one can discover) contribute his gifts to lifting the College back. His heart was not (to be frank) in his new and noble

1 The Prince possessed a copy of the 1775 Quarto of the Manx Bible, now in the Library of the Manx Museum.

2 Years afterwards when Prince Lucien unveiled at Penzance the monument he had erected at his own expense to Dolly Pentreath, then supposed to be the last who had spoken the old Cornish language, Brown attended and was greeted with 'How do you do, Mr Brown? You taught me once how to eat porridge'.

College, to elevate it: the iron had entered his soul, and he had no longer a son of Oxford's love or desire to increase, for her sake, her glory; that desire which curiously persists, deserved, in so many of her far less deserving sons who have acknowledged, through life, her influence.

Brown, thought Dr Fowler, 'never took kindly to the life of an Oxford Fellow'. 'I have no wish', he had written as an undergraduate to Archdeacon Moore, 'to fatten on a Fellowship'; and again, 'An Oxford tutorship does not attract me'; and after a few terms of private pupils he began to yearn for his native Island, where his mother's house had been clouded with sorrow by the death of a sister. He had dreams, too, of doing something for the Island which would perpetuate his name there. But there was a yet stronger reason. Later on, when asked why he had wanted to return, he replied in dialect, 'What was the for I left England? It was the longin' for the lil Island that done the *jeel* on me,[1] and besides, la, wasn' theer a gel over at Ramsey that was haulin' and pullin' at my heart strings like the very mischief like'? And so, although his ability had attracted the attention of Mr Gladstone and he had tempting offers to enter the public service, and in spite of the opportunities which Oxford afforded, he decided to apply for the Vice-Principalship of King William's College, which had become vacant in 1855. That he had been assisted to some extent by the Barrow Scholarship, intended to help young Manxmen to train for service in the Manx Church, no doubt weighed heavily with Brown's sense of honour in making this decision. He had recently been ordained by Wilberforce, Bishop of Oxford.[2]

[1] 'We are all Manx people together, and I want you to feel how intensely Manx we are.... You, when you go away have the "longing". Oh, it is a terrible thing, this longing. I assure you it has been at the root of everything I have done in connection with Manx literature.... There was a gel at home at Kirk Braddan, in the Vicarage there, and she was longin', and she must go back to Kirk Marown. It was only the next parish, but she must go back. "And why?" said the Misthress. "Oh, I'm longin'." "But what are you longin' for?" "The cows", she said.' (From a Speech at Laxey, December, 1895.)

[2] He did not, however, proceed to Priest's Orders until late in life.

IV

Behind other reasons for this move of Brown's lay a romantic
ambition—call it a young man's dream—of making the Manx nation
a small but vivid centre of culture, to spread its light abroad even as,
many centuries before, the candlelight of Bede's monastery had
thrown its beams from Jarrow down the length of England and
across to Europe. Some sentences he wrote in applying for the post
will indicate his hopes—

My principal motive is the discharge of a duty which I owe to the
Island of my birth, and to the place of my education. Should it be
in my power to promote the cause of sound Christian education in
the Isle of Man (than which I am deeply conscious that no other
can be effectual for the real improvement of our common country),
I shall deem myself singularly happy in having used my humble
ability in communicating to such a movement any healthy impulse,
however partial, however inchoate. And I trust that you will not
consider me guilty of presumption when I say that five years spent
partly in practical conformity to, partly in familiar and experimental
study of, the great educational problems as seeking their solution in
one of the largest, and most advantageous fields of enquiry, viz. the
University of Oxford, must at least have awakened me to the
difficulties attendant upon the task upon which I am at present
desirous of being engaged, even if they have not prepared me for
the satisfactory performance of it.

My position as Vice-principal of King William's would appear to
me to be eminently *Insular*. And to *Insular* authorities I hope this
idea may be anything rather than a disqualification. That the energies
of an Insular College should mainly terminate in the Island I have
long felt; that the Isle of Man is the legitimate sphere of its operations,
I should think, cannot be doubted.

So far then as my subordinate endeavours would go, my aim
would be to bring the College to bear (if possible) mainly on the
Isle of Man, to use it (if possible) as a lever by which the education
of the Island generally might be elevated.

I trust that you will not regard these projects as visionary. Viewing them (as I cannot but do) as eminently practical, eminently Insular, eminently Manx, I cannot but think that they must commend themselves to every lover of his Native Island: and that in accepting and enunciating such projects the Trustees would secure the hearty sympathies of all Manxmen.

He was elected, and started his career at King William's with these aspirations, full of high hope; strengthened, in 1857, by his marriage with his cousin Emilia Stowell of Ramsey.[1] The records of the bachelor interval before this tell of hard work (he contributed several articles, signed T. E. B., to Dr William Smith's *Dictionary of the Bible*); of new teaching methods, happy discourses with his pupils, holidays in which he took them for College runs or on early fishing expeditions (he knew how to handle a boat in a strong breeze); or of evenings filled with talk and music; of tramps to hold special services in various parts of the Island; of new acquaintances too, including the great George Borrow, who asseverated to him that the view from Maughold Head was one of the finest in the British Isles.[2] Brown repaid Borrow by drawing his attention to the existence of Manx *Carvals*. Another acquaintance of those days was old George Wood, who had watched over Napoleon at St Helena. Wood, the son of a former Governor of the Isle of Man, had retired thither to devote his life to metaphysics. He was a pure idealist, and his talks with Brown would invariably turn upon Berkeley. The time was happy enough in its way. But King William's College failed to develope according to his extravagant expectations. His own pupilage there had been (as happens in every school) a time of exceptional and

1 The wedding ceremony was performed by his friend Dr Fowler in Kirk Maughold Church.

2 Brown accompanied Borrow, with Dr Dixon, to the house in which Archibald Cregeen, author of the *Manx Dictionary*, was born. It was then used as an inn. On entering, Borrow removed his hat. 'Oh, Sir', said the landlady, 'you had better keep your hat on', Dr Dixon adding, 'Oh, yes, Mr Borrow, keep your hat on'. Borrow arose to his full tremendous height. 'Keep my hat on? Never, in the house where the great Cregeen was born!'

misleading brilliance, and Canon Wilson records very frankly and faithfully the subsequent ebb of its fortune.[1] This had by no means been stayed by the publication of Farrar's *Eric: or Little by Little*, in 1858. We are familiar enough nowadays with the unction some ex-Public School novelists display in fouling their own nests: but it was then a novelty, and it did King William's College no good. Looking back upon it in a lecture on *Castletown Fifty Years Ago*, given in 1895, Brown says:

Farrar did us harm. He published a book called *Eric*. It was a foolish book. It was about a boy at a public school, and the school he indicated was King William's College, though he did not give it that name. It was a grossly exaggerated picture. I put it to any King William's College man whatever, whether he could recognise the College in the description as given in *Eric*. I was there precisely at that time. By some lamentable accident or twist to the good Archdeacon's mind, or something in his experience that went wrong about that time, he produced this deplorable book. We repudiated it with indignation. It was not a perfect school. Where is there such? I have had a good deal to do with schools and never found a perfect school any more than I have found a perfect boy or perfect man; but I think King William's College did well, and trained up some excellent men for the service of God in Church and State.

But one gathers that the Governing Body of the College had small enthusiasm for Brown's reforms or sympathy with his perhaps extravagant hopes; and in 1861 he severed his connection with it; accepting the position of Headmaster of the Crypt School, Gloucester, and celebrating his departure by a walking tour around the Island and a paper on *Scholastic Pedestrianism*, contributed to an insular newspaper.

Brown's connection with the Crypt School, Gloucester—afterwards generally referred to by him as the 'Gloucester Episode'—turned out disappointingly. The School had been founded early in

1 See Appendix I, p. 76.

the sixteenth century by a burgess of the City of Gloucester for the education of certain poor boys: but its inability to compete with the more flourishing Cathedral School had induced the Governors, before he entered on the mastership, to make certain reforms of which he disapproved from the first. One gathers also that ('jus' the shy') he found certain publicities of life there a torture to his Island reserve. He was unhappy at any rate; his tenure of the post was brief; and his letters of this period contain little of interest. We may note only a visit to the Great Exhibition of 1862, described by him as 'this bewildering mad-house of the Arts'; his enjoyment of the Musical Festival; and the delight of an excursion in the Forest of Dean.

To HIS MOTHER

21 *September* 1862

The Festival was a great treat. We enjoyed the Oratorio very much; we had excellent places, and could both see and hear to advantage. It was my favourite, the *Elijah*.... When H. and A. were in London, we had a geological excursion in the Dean Forest. The day was glorious: we got some specimens, and partially disinterred a very extraordinary skull, the teeth of which — has taken to Cambridge.... Then we rambled out of the forest on to a common high up in the hills, where I had the inexpressible delight of lying down on a bed of heather in full bloom(!!!), with harebells and even gorse close by. This was the crowning triumph. — was 'visibly affected', as I told him; for he loves the I. of Man and the nature of its scenery. I only wish I had gone there earlier in the day and by myself! What a treat it would have been, what inward communing, what memories, what dead hopes and fears, leaves that have faded from my tree of life!! And over all was the bright sky, blue as the harebell itself, and bluer; and, as it always is, circumscribing all our littleness of life, larger and better than it. Moreover I ate some blackberries: but they were poor and flavourless compared with the Manx ones.

And this reminds me that to-day we have had a mulberry pudding off our own tree. We thought to compare it with a blackberry one; but wae's me! what a difference! We all agreed that it was immensely inferior to our old friend.... Baby is becoming a songstress; perhaps the Festival has shed some occult influence upon her....Your description of the view from Douglas Head makes my mouth water. Glorious, indeed, it must be now.

The one remarkable fact to chronicle of this 'Gloucester Episode' is that he had the early training of a boy of genius, William Ernest Henley, who has left us this record of his indebtedness to Brown:

His teaching opened to me ways of thought and speech that came upon me like a call from the world outside—the great, quick, living world—and discovered me the beginnings, the true materials of myself....The matter of that purpose is that he was T. E. Brown, the man of genius, the first ever seen; and being so, he took hold upon me, with a grip that he never knew, and led me out into the nearer distances—into the shallows at the edge of the great sea—to a point I might never have reached without him. What he did for me, practically, was to suggest such possibilities in life and character as I had never dreamed.

Boy and Master parted, not to meet until thirty years later, when Henley, as Editor of *The National Observer*, had the privilege of publishing many of the loveliest of Brown's marvellous autumnal lyrics.

In 1860 at Clifton, the beautiful suburb of Bristol, a Company had been formed for the purpose of establishing a school distinguished by a wider range of studies and more specialisation than other schools allowed; more opportunity for varied abilities; but with the general ideal of a Public School as a place for forming character and training faculties. Clifton College was opened on September the 30th, 1862, with sixty boys. The first Headmaster appointed had resigned before taking up his duties; and that great schoolmaster, John Percival, who had for two years worked under Temple of Rugby, was chosen in his stead.

Canon J. M. Wilson shall tell, on a later page,[1] how he was asked by Percival if he knew of someone to take over the Modern

1 Appendix I.

Side of the new School; how he named Brown, and arranged an interview; and how, after a somewhat extraordinary evening, Percival decided 'Oh, he'll do!' Before settling the matter, however, the two men had another interview, this time in Oxford; and there, writes Percival,

As chance would have it, I met him standing at the corner of St Mary's Entry, in a somewhat Johnsonian attitude, four-square, his hands deep in his pockets to keep himself still, and looking decidedly *volcanic*.

We very soon came to terms, and I left him there under promise to come to Clifton as my colleague at the beginning of the following Term; and, needless to say, St Mary's Entry has had an additional interest to me ever since.

Sometimes I have wondered, and it would be worth a good deal to know, what thoughts were coursing through that richly furnished, teeming brain as he stood there by St Mary's Church, with Oriel College in front of him—thoughts of his own struggles and triumphs, and of all the great souls that had passed to and fro over the pavement around him; and all set in the lurid background of the undergraduate life to which he had been condemned as a servitor at ChristChurch.

So—like many another poor man who has to take up such work as comes to hand—in September, 1863, Brown accepted a new chance and began his career at Clifton. The College flourished from the start. In the first two years it quadrupled its numbers (it has since come to average about 700 boys), and in 1864 the authorities established Boarding Houses. H. G. Dakyns, who had joined the staff in 1862, waived his seniority and T. E. B. took charge of 'Brown's House', which he ruled from 1864 to 1892. (Afterwards, from 1895 to 1907, it was governed by W. W. Asquith, whose brother became in time Prime Minister and subsequently Earl of Oxford.) Of other notable friends among his colleagues were E. M. Oakeley, brother of Sir Herbert Oakeley and a no less devout musician, G. H. Wollaston, A. M. Worthington and Sidney Irwin, who afterwards edited Brown's *Letters*. I suppose it is allowable, at this distance of time, to describe these and other early Clifton Masters as a queer crew; possessing, man for man, extraordinary individual parts. Indeed, going forward to the year 1881 or thereabouts, one may say that we boys considered most of them as more than a little mad. There was one, for instance, who, if you were guilty of a false concord, would rush at you and drive you to take shelter behind the desk in fear of being hacked on the shins. Another, when the School Marshal came around with the 'list', would be surprised on his knees, invoking the ventilator while he illustrated the proper uses of *ipse, se, ille, iste*, by some such prayer as '*He* prays to Apollo that *He* will deliver *him* from *these* fellows'. A third in a moment of irritation would tell his entire class, 'Gentlemen, there is only one name for you. Singly and collectively you are Bilge'. Great wits at any rate were frequently allied on those premises with eccentricity, to say the least of it; and Percival indeed seemed to have chosen them for that quality—wisely because, while they made life amusing, he, as Head, could always control them to a common purpose and tradition. How rapidly that tradition was established other witnesses may testify; but within twenty years (as the present writer can affirm) the *ethos* of Clifton had rooted itself as firmly as though Clifton had stood for centuries; and its main characteristics were freedom and curiosity of the mind tempered by a severe conscience in all matters of service and obedience to Duty—

Stern daughter of the voice of God—

above all, repressing any tendency in the individual to 'side' or swagger. The reader may perhaps the better appreciate this if it be added that the School proudly remembers the late Field-Marshal Earl Haig (who entered it in 1877), not only for his fame but as a typical son.[1] Those early years, of course, were tentative and full of

1 I feel that the School at this time of day, conscious of present strength and promise, may easily have heard enough about Percival's time and its reputed Paladins. But let the generation be patient: it also will, in its turn, come to talk of its age as Homeric, or perhaps better.

experiments, in all of which Brown took his share; in the building up of school sports, especially Cricket, Handfives and Athletics (even a Boat Club was started on the Avon, but lasted no long time). And these sports so prospered that in the Oxford and Cambridge match of 1878 all the twenty Cambridge wickets were taken by three Cliftonian bowlers, and in 1881 Clifton felt as proud, probably, of having contributed to Oxford the President of its Boat Club and the Captains of its Cricket and Rugby Football teams as, later, in the Great War, of having an old Cliftonian in command of each of the three main fronts of the British Army.

Brown also helped to found the College choir, the 'Cecilian' choir, and other musical societies, and gave much assistance in compiling the College Hymn Book, to which he contributed a noble Hymn for Ascension Day.

But it is time to turn from his scholastic activities to some record of his domestic life during these years: concluding this section with the testimony of Mr Horatio F. Brown, one of the many boys who passed through Clifton in that time and afterwards achieved distinction. It confirms that of W. E. Henley already quoted.

The circumstances in which I came to be taught by T. E. Brown were exceptional. I and some other boys were going in for History Scholarships at Oxford. The Headmaster allowed us to attend a special history class under T. E. Brown.

My recollection is that his was the most vivid teaching I ever received: great width of view and poetical, almost passionate, power of presentment. For example, we were reading Froude's *History*, and I shall never forget how it was Brown's words, Brown's voice, not the historian's, that made me feel the great democratic function which the monasteries performed in England; the view became alive in his mouth. Again the same thing happened when we came to the Reformation as it showed itself at Oxford; the vivid presentment of the passions moving both sides in the controversy, and the lively picturing of details (e.g. the Gloucester Hall scholar escaping over heavy ploughed fields), all set forth with such dramatic force, and aided by a splendid voice, left an indelible impression on my mind.

He had such an appreciation of style too! I remember that we were reading what was then thought to be an exceptionally dry and tough work, Hallam's *Constitutional History*. The way in which he delivered the passage beginning, 'But lest the spectre of indefeasible right should stand once more in arms on the tomb of the house of York', not only fixed for ever the historical importance of the event that Hallam was discussing, but, as it were, let me into Hallam himself, put one on terms of intelligence with the historian. Of course it was all there before, in the book itself, and other people had said it all, time and time again; but for me it was Brown's voice, Brown's perception, that made it real.... He never spoke to me out of school, and I never knew him at all privately or socially at that time: but his personality made a great impression; his slow sort of urgent walk, like Leviathan, his thick massive figure, above all his voice. I used to see him in the distance on his lonely strolls about the downs, and his figure seemed to belong to, and to explain the downs, the river, the woods, the Severn, and the far Welsh hills. I remember him walking in the rain, and looking as if he liked it, as I did. Personally, at that time I was afraid of him; but he stirred fancy, curiosity, imagination. I should say that his educational function lay in 'widening'....

V

The record of a Schoolmaster's alternations between work and holidays affords as a rule no more interest to the reader than that of shiftings (as the Vicar of Wakefield put it) 'from the blue bed to the brown': and T. E. B.'s holidays were mainly pedestrian in a double sense. But some notes may be inserted here, mainly compiled from recollections which his surviving daughters and his niece, Miss Ethel Stowell Brown, have kindly allowed to be used in this volume.

The family usually spent their holidays at Keswick, with a slice kept for a visit to the Isle of Man and an occasional trip abroad (oftenest to Switzerland) for Brown himself in company with one of the Clifton Masters or some other friend. One almost feels that Brown delighted in Keswick chiefly because the summits around gave him a view of his own little Island, his purple hesperid—'Aw!

there she is, the darlin'!'—and indeed few sights in England can compare for romantic charm with that of 'little Mona'—say from the top of Scafell—lying like a shield, with Snaefell for boss, upon the western ocean against the sunset.

> Look, look! as through a sliding panel
> Of pearl, our Mona! Has she crossed the Channel
> For us, that there she lies almost
> A portion of the Cambrian coast?
> Dark purple peaks against the sun,
> A gorgeous thing to look upon?
> Nay, darling of my soul! I fear
> To see your beauty come so near—
> I would not have it! This is not your rest—
> Go back, go back, into your Golden West!

'Let's *gup* ['go up'] Skiddaw!' (or Helvellyn or Great Gable, as it might be) he would suddenly suggest at the breakfast table, and often on the way up would stop to have a bathe in one of the lovely 'dubs'. The younger members of the party greatly envied their Mother, who could climb like a chamois; but the pace was usually set by that of a maiden aunt, who would never remain at the foot of anything, however steep ('You go on! I'll just take m' time') and had to be encouraged by a trail of gooseberries laid by the graceless youngsters. On off days the family used to go on Derwentwater in a stout old tub of a boat. The maiden aunt could row, and would pull a bow oar to Brown's stroke, but was no adept in keeping time.

Our progress was marked by *crash!* from the aunt's oar, ' *Murder!* ' from my father. *Crash bang!* from the aunt, ' *Murder! !* ' (crescendo) from my father: loud exclamations from the united family, each one trying to explain to the aunt the art of keeping time, while she, still crashing, demanded placidly: 'What are ye all shouting about?'

There would appear indeed to have been a family 'Saga of the Aunts', from which the famous Lobster Episode may here be quoted. It happened in the Isle of Man. T. E. B. and his daughter Ethel went on a visit to the 'A(u)nt Hill'. The Aunts had purchased a lobster to do honour to the occasion. While the meal was preparing Aunt Major entered in consternation to say that she could *not* put the poor creature into boiling water: it was walking about the table hissing at her, and tears were in its eyes! (Indeed, in later editions, its claws were being clasped in supplication.) Miss Ethel begged her to desist, then, as anyway all shellfish were poison to her father—a suggestion scouted by Aunt Minor: 'Chut! How could a nice fresh lobster hurt anyone? I'll soon put it in the pot'. The matter was referred to Brown who would have none of the poor beast. In triumph Aunt Major removed it to the garden, where it was tethered all night to a gooseberry bush. (Later editions mention a red ribbon to match its complexion; but this must be consigned amongst the *errata* as, having escaped the pot, the creature still wore its native hue.) Next morning Aunt Major loudly announced to the sleeping household that 'The poor beast had *fainted*!' Hereupon the other Aunt appeared at the window with T. E. B.'s seawater bath and flopped the contents over the sufferer. A scream from Aunt Major, 'There! You've *drowned* it now!' Sleepy voice of T. E. B. within, praying that 'this poor creature need not be reported through *all* its vicissitudes'. In vain! The Aunts continued to play Greek Chorus till Aunt Major ended by carefully escorting it back to Alice the Fishwife, and was not satisfied till she had made a space amid a pile of struggling lobsters and 'restored it to its companions'.

Innocent hilarity of this kind diversified the holidays: but during Term life at 34, College Road, Clifton, moved quietly enough. Miss Dora Brown's earliest memories begin there.

The three youngest in the nursery (the others being at school) were my brother Braddan, six years old, myself four years, my brother Hugh, barely three.

Little Braddan ruled us rather strictly. He was a fine bonny child and I have the most vivid picture at this moment of his saving my life when my pinafore caught fire, as we three little wretches stretched over the nursery guard dangling long strings into the fire: my pinafore blazed up, Braddan instantly tore it off, stamped on it and hid it under the bed.

Next day it was discovered, and I remember our utter astonishment at not being scolded when, by dint of putting two and two together, our elders made out what actually took place.[1]

The next tiny incident that emerges from the cloudy past was my decision to call my new doll 'Betsy Lee', I did not know why, but I had heard a great deal about her, and thought it very suitable. I can see now my father and mother exchanging smiles!

Naturally we saw very little of my father during busy term time. If in the evenings as we grew older he joined the family party, we were trained to sit as still as mice not to disturb him. Luckily we were devoted to reading, and this kept us happy.

Even as a tiny child one of my deep impressions was the intense affection between my father and mother.

She was the most wonderful help to him in every way, her wisdom, and patience, her merriment, tenderness and camaraderie making and sustaining him: level-headed, a good manager of her household. She had been one of a large family (a doctor's) in Ramsey, Isle of Man, and had been taken away early from school to help in housework at home. She indeed adapted herself marvellously to her new sphere of life.

As a House-master Brown was, to adapt a phrase of Wellington's, 'much exposed to parents', and often had to summon his truly fine manners to correct his irascibility. Towards the poor, or towards his social inferiors, these manners were constantly perfect. His niece, Miss Stowell, notes an instance:

In our early days a nice old woman used to come to the house to help in the replenishing of our wardrobes. She came by the day and had her midday meal with us. On one of these occasions T. E. B. was a beloved guest at our table, and when old Mrs T. rose up after the meal to return to the workroom, he also rose and held the door open for her with the same grace that he would have shown to a

---

[1] The death of this little son Braddan, in April, 1876, at the age of seven, dealt Brown a wound past solace. No comment is needed on it here, the father's anguish being disclosed (perhaps too distressfully) in the series of poems entitled *Aber Stations*.

duchess. The old woman herself was quite overcome by the act and
was found shedding copious tears to think that the 'strange gentleman' should have shown so much condescension!

'If I lose my manners', Mr Irwin quotes him as saying once over
some trivial forgetfulness, 'what is to become of me?'

I, who edit this Memoir, may here interpose a personal anecdote;
since it once fell to me—a blundering innocent in the hands of fate—
to put those manners to severest proof. A candidate for a Scholarship
at Clifton, awkward, and abominably conscious of it, and sensitive,
I had been billeted on Brown's hospitality without his knowledge.
The mistake (I cannot tell who was responsible) could not be
covered out of sight; it was past all aid of kindly dissimulation by
the time Brown returned to the house to find the unwelcome guest
bestowed in his drawing-room. I had taken up a book from the
table—Whymper's *Scrambles Among the Alps*—and was lost in its
pages when I heard the front door open, an explanatory voice
(female) in the hall, and then, as a French stage-direction might put
it, *détonation à la cantonade*—'What! What is it you're saying?...
Murder! Who sent him?...I'll have none of it!' (More gentle
explanation.) 'Oh, very well....But I won't have this fellow from
Heaven knows where contaminating the morals of my boys! Since
you've admitted him, my dear, you'll just have to put up with him
as one of the family!...' The drawing-room door burst open, and
I confronted him, standing and trembling, 'Whymper' in one hand
and my note of introduction in the other. Followed a dreadful
pause, and then in a strangely softened voice, which I shall always
remember for its music, 'Are you fond of climbing?'—and when
I confessed that I knew nothing about it, but wanted to—'Ah, but
no Switzerland for you yet! When the time comes you must begin
with Cumberland!' Thus was I admitted into the family circle.
Miss Dora, at that time a small child, is good enough to remember
the visitor and describes him as 'pale, smiling, clever, very quiet....
I remember very few boys who ever stayed with us, but Q stands

out in my memory, though I don't think he ever spoke to us'.
I don't remember smiling or being clever; but the reader will admit
that I had every reason to be pale and very quiet.

Very early next morning there came a rap at my door, and the
voice of my host enquiring, 'Would I like to get up and take an
early walk?' I dressed in a hurry, and we went out together upon
Durdham (or, as he chose to call them, Durdleaen) Downs—

> By the Avon's side,
> Where tall rocks flank the winding tide.
> There come when morning's virgin kiss
> Awakes from dreams the clematis,
> And every thorn and briar is set
> As with a diamond coronet.

As we walked and I drank in the beauty of this morning's scene,
all fresh as it was novel, Brown swung round upon me with 'I come
here every morning before breakfast. Why, d'ye think.... You'd
never guess it—taking me for a high and dry old Scholar, I suppose?
But I come out here to make *poetry*'; adding, very shyly and
whimsically ('jus' the shy'), 'Yes, yes, to make poetry—or try—if
you'll believe it'. Thereafter and for the rest of my stay he treated
me with a consideration so quiet and pleasant, so easy yet attentive,
that his dearest friend or most distinguished visitor could not have
demanded more.

Hitherto this Memoir has said little or nothing of Brown's poetry;
and for the sufficient reason that hitherto—with the exception of *Betsy
Lee*, published by Messrs Macmillan in 1873, with no author's name
—none of it had appeared in print. But rumours of it soon began
to spread; and the writer remembers Brown's coming to Dakyns'
House one evening and reciting *Tommy Big-Eyes* or *Christmas Rose*
to the boys—I cannot remember which; for these performances,
later, became fairly frequent. In 1881 Macmillans published *Fo'c's'le
Yarns*, under the author's name. A second edition followed in 1889.
Meanwhile Messrs Swan Sonnenschein and Co. had published in

1887 *The Doctor and other Poems.* This volume bore his name, as
did also *The Manx Witch and other Poems*, in 1889, and *Old John
and other Poems*, in 1893. The two last-named volumes were published by Messrs Macmillan.

But an estimate of Brown's poetry must be deferred to a later
section.

Many have asked, and Brown, by many an occasional word in
his talk and his writing, has encouraged the question, 'Was he happy
in his many years' work at Clifton?' On the whole, and with some
reservation we may say 'yes'—'yes', although in the end he escaped
from it gladly and enjoyed his escape. One side of him, no doubt,
loathed formality, routine, Masters'-meetings above all; he was, as
he defiantly proclaimed himself, a nature-loving, somewhat in-
tractable Kelt; and if one may hint at a fault in him, it was that now
and then he soon *tired.* A man so spendthrift of emotion is bound
at times to knock on the bottom of his emotional coffers; and no
doubt he was true *to a mood* when he wrote:

> I'm here at Clifton, grinding at the mill
>   My feet for thrice nine barren years have trod,
> But there are rocks and waves at Scarlett still,
>   And gorse runs riot in Glen Chass—thank God!
>
> Alert, I seek exactitude of rule,
>   I step and square my shoulders with the squad,
> But there are blaeberries on old Barrule,
>   And Langness has its heather still—thank God!

—with the rest of the rebellious stanzas. We may go farther and allow
that he played with the mood until he sometimes forgot on which
side lay seriousness and on which side humour. Still it *was* a mood;
and it was Brown, after all, who wrote *Planting*.

> Who would be planted chooseth not the soil
> Or here or there,
> Or loam or peat,
> Wherein he best may grow

And bring forth guerdon of the planter's toil—
The lily is most fair,
But says not—'I will only blow
Upon a southern land'; the cedar makes no coil
What rock shall owe
The springs that wash his feet;
The crocus cannot arbitrate the foil
That for his purple radiance is most meet—
Lord, even so
I ask one prayer,
The which if it be granted,
It skills not where
Thou plantest me, only I would be planted.

You don't care for school-work [he writes to an Old Cliftonian].
. . . I demur to your statement that when you take up schoolmastering
your leisure for this kind of thing will be practically gone. Not at
all. If you have the root of the matter in you the school-work will
insist upon this kind of thing as a relief. My plan always was to
recognise two lives as necessary—the one the outer Kapelistic life
of drudgery, the other the inner and cherished life of the spirit.
It is true that the one has a tendency to kill the other, but it must
not, and you must see that it does not. . . . The pedagogic is needful
for bread and butter, also for a certain form of joy; of the inner life
you know what I think.

These are wise words, and I believe they represent Brown more
truly than utterances which only seem more genuine because less
deliberate. He excelled as a Housemaster, with an excellence not
achieveable by men whose hearts are removed from their work: he
engendered and enjoyed fervent friendships and the enthusiastic
admiration of many youngsters: he must have known of these
enthusiasms, and was not the man to condemn them: he had an
abiding assurance of assisting in that success of Clifton which he
certainly respected. To the whole School he had become, in the
days when I knew it, an 'institution', the beneficence of which
(unless memory play me false) depended less on any personal 'touch'
with the boys, than in his gusto for teaching, his enthusiasm for

sound learning of any kind, and a general sense among us that in him we possessed something great. In 1879 Dr Percival had been appointed President of Trinity College, Oxford; and the Governors of the College appointed James Maurice Wilson (Brown's old friend) to succeed him. Possibly, for reasons which the reader may gather, Brown, with his many incomparable qualities, was passed over; but this, so far from causing resentment, disturbed him not at all. He wrote to Wilson, urging him to come—and Wilson came.

Brown went on serving Clifton loyally. He longed, indeed, for the day of emancipation, to return to his Island; he was impatient; but one must decline to believe he was unhappy. Indeed, his presence sufficiently denied it. How shall I describe him? A sturdy, thick-set figure, inclining to rotundity, yet athletic; a face extraordinarily mobile; bushy, grey eyebrows; eyes at once deeply and radiantly human, yet holding the primitive faun in their coverts; a broad mouth made for broad, natural laughter, hearty without lewdness. 'There are nice Rabelaisians, and there are nasty; but the latter are not Rabelaisians.' 'I have an idea', he claimed, 'that my judgment within this area is infallible.' And it was. All honest laughter he welcomed as a Godlike function.

> God sits upon His hill,
> And sees the shadows fly;
> And if He laughs at fools, why should He not?

And for that matter, why should not we? But at this point his fine manners intervened, correcting, counselling moderation. 'I am certain God made fools for us to enjoy, but there must be *an economy of joy* in the presence of a fool; you must not betray your enjoyment.' Imagine all this overlaid with a certain portliness of bearing, suggestive of the high-and-dry Oxford scholar. Add something of the parsonic;[1] add a simple natural piety which purged the parsonic of all 'churchiness'.

---

1 Although ordained Deacon before leaving Oxford, Brown did not proceed to Priestly Orders until 1885, and then, characteristically for the sake of being

This silence and solitude are to me absolute food [he writes from the Clifton College Library on the morning of Christmas Day, 1875], especially after all the row and worry at the end of Term.... Where are the men and women? Well, now look here, you'll not mention it again. They're all in Church. See how good God is! See how He has placed these leitourgic traps in which people, especially disagreeable people, get caught—and lo! the universe for me!!! me—me....

The moral of his life residing rather in what the man was than in what he did, many have tried to describe the essential Brown of those days, and indeed the temptation to describe this indescribable could scarcely be resisted. But perhaps his old Headmaster, Percival (who had, as many of his Sermons attest, a great gift for the illuminating phrase), has hit on the right word—'volcanic', and goes to the Bay of Naples to fetch home a simile for him:

We can find plenty of beauty in the familiar northern scenes; but we miss the pent-up forces, the volcanic outbursts, the tropic glow, and all the surprising manifold and tender and sweet-scented outpourings of soil and sunshine, so spontaneous, so inexhaustibly rich, and with the heat of a great fire burning and palpitating underneath all the time.[1]

Another of his colleagues wrote, 'It must be admitted that when Brown was on his legs making a speech, or even delivering a Sermon, anything might happen. On one occasion he gave an imaginary conversation between St Paul and Matthew Arnold, not favourable to the author of *Religion and Dogma*. Next day he showed me his written Sermon—an unexceptionable discourse, but only half of it

useful in helping with the services of the Mission of St Barnabas, which the College had set up in one of the poorer quarters of Bristol. It is not generally known that on the death of Archdeacon Moore, February, 1886, Brown was offered the vacant post and at first was inclined to accept. He wrote to his old pupil, Rev. F. Lamothe, who had been curate to Archdeacon Moore at Andreas for eleven years, asking him to remain. 'You will do the parish work, Fred, and I will sit at the desk.' When, however, he heard of the objections raised on account of the unconventional language of the *Fo'c's'le Yarns*, he withdrew.

1 *Oxford Magazine*, November the 3rd, 1897.

was in the Sermon he preached'. Dr Boas on p. 111 tells the story
of his famous Sunday lecture on Hymns. As Charles Cannan—Head
of Brown's House—afterwards reported it to me, at the close of the
hymn and after a long pause, Brown's voice spoke his exordium,
slowly repeating—

> From Greenland's icy mountains,
> From India's coral strand,
> Where Afric's sunny fountains
> Roll down their golden sand...

(Another impressive pause); then—'We owe this imagery to a
Bishop' (pause): 'But the imagery is cheap, and can have cost the
Bishop very little'! With all his Sunday evening addresses in Big
School it was the same: anything might happen but the immediately
expected. He would start upon some such subject as Bishop Hooker,
and within five minutes it was odds that one might be listening to a
story of the Peel Lifeboat, or to some comment or illustration,
for the moment apparently fetched out of nowhere but even in
the shock of surprise revealing itself as relevant, and more—as
memorably apposite.

And there it was; and we had to take Brown as he gave himself
to us. We were at least as proud of him as Etonians of the author of
Ionica. But no comparisons will serve. Falstaffian—with a bent of
homely piety; Johnsonian—with a fiery Keltic heat and a passionate
adoration of Nature: all such epithets fail as soon as they are uttered.
The man was at once absolute and Protean: entirely sincere, and yet
a different being to each separate friend. 'There was no getting to
the end of Brown.'

In April, 1881, his health began to give cause for anxiety. He was
exhausted with work, and went to Seaton in South Devon for a rest;
thence to Switzerland, with three months' leave of absence—'a
pleasant and restorative time'. The end of 1882 was saddened for
him by the death of his brother Alfred, 'a very sweet-tempered,
kindly man, of great moral strength and self control'. In May, 1883,

he visited Lugano and, a little later, his old College, Oriel, where he sat at table and talked with another ex-Fellow, Cardinal Newman. The summer vacation was spent with his family and the Wilsons in Cumberland, his greatest delight being to teach his youngest daughter Dora, aged twelve, to climb with him. In the following year, 1884, he was again granted three months' holiday, of which he spent five weeks in the Isle of Man, the remainder being devoted to climbing in the Lakes, where his friend Dakyns accompanied him part of the time. Holidays in January, 1885, were divided between the Isle of Wight, Italy and Keswick; where, in a lonely place on the hills, he so badly sprained his ankle as to be laid up for several months, during which time he occupied his mind with reading Petrarch, Ariosto and other Italian classics, as well as re-reading many old Greek and Latin and English favourites.

In February, 1886, his brother, Hugh Stowell Brown, died suddenly at his home in Liverpool. T. E. B. vastly admired this famous brother. He wrote to a friend, that 'to hear him in conversation was a treat; I have never met such a conversationalist anywhere—his fund of anecdote; his lightning wit, his declamation, sometimes alarming'. He had often heard his brother's Sermons, which were full of terrific power, while his lectures were extremely witty and racy. 'He has ringed me round all my life with moral strength and abettance. I hardly know how much. What is it? Not direct control nor suggestion but a sort of taking each other for granted.'

Brown spent his holidays this year at Penmaenmawr (climbing Tryfaen 'using hands and knees as much as feet'); and in the Isle of Man. In October he had a letter from his friend Mr (now Sir) Hall Caine (for whom he had, both as a critic and a Manxman, unbounded admiration), asking his opinion on the plot of a Manx story, sketched in outline. Brown answered that he did not think the scene could be placed in the Isle of Man or timed in the nineteenth century. But when the story eventually became *The Deemster* he confessed himself amazed at the skill with which the author had overcome both difficulties. He himself, just then, was musing over the story of *The Manx Witch*, and Macmillans were planning to publish *The Doctor*. His admiration for Hall Caine was a lasting one: it came to its height over *The Manxman*, the genius and essential purity of which he was ready to defend against all comers, and never ceased to extol. But it is a ticklish business to praise the living, and what Hall Caine thought of Brown may be read in the Appendix with which he has honoured this volume.

It was while on a climbing expedition among the Lakes in the summer of 1887 that Brown first noticed indications of his wife's failing strength, as she had to halt for rest at every twenty yards. And the year 1888 brought misfortune early: for in January he broke his right arm while playing Fives—a trifle in comparison with the next shock, when shortly afterwards his wife's fatal illness declared itself. He had adored her, even as a friend remarked (unjustly) almost to the exclusion of their children. Yet in the midst of mental anguish and spiritual perturbation he could write to a friend in like case—the Rev. E. W. Kissack—the following triumphant confession of a faith established after years of questioning:

One thing emerges—my absolute belief in immortality. I am not naturally a materialist; that is a plant not native to my mind; but scales of materialism have sometimes grown upon my eyes. They now vanish utterly, and I am dazzled and confounded by the inevitable presence, the close connatural rebound of the belief. I have always been an idealist, subject to the dim spots of material feculence that from time to time have obscured my vision. Now I feel my body to be nothing but an integument, and the inveteracy of the material association to be a tie little more than momentary and quite casual.... Death is the key to another room, and it is the very next room.

And afterwards:

My dear fellow-sufferer, what is it after all? Why this sinking of the heart, this fainting, sorrowing of the spirit? There is no separation: life is continuous. All that was stable and good, good and therefore stable, in our union with the loved one, is unquestionably permanent, will endure for ever. It cannot be otherwise.... When love has done its full work, has wrought soul into soul so that every fibre has become part of the common life—*quis separabit?* Can you conceive yourself as existing at all without *her?* No, you can't; well, then, it follows that you don't, and never will.

His wife died on July the 3rd, 1888, and straightway after the funeral Brown went to Ullswater, where he wanted to be alone to wander over the Cumberland mountains. The summer of 1889 found him again on a visit to the Island, of which one adventure may be recorded. One Sunday he attended an indoor service at Old Kirk Braddan, while simultaneously another service was being held in the Churchyard for a multitude of summer visitors. Brown could never reconcile himself to these fashionable open-air services; and on this occasion he noted, with sardonic glee, that while the preacher inside was holding forth on the subject of Judas Iscariot, in through the open windows poured the stentorian chorus 'Crown Him, crown Him, crown Him Lord of All!' In October of this year, after Brown's return to Clifton by way of Keswick, occurred the wreck of the Norwegian ship *St George*, and the rescue of her crew by the Peel Lifeboat, the story of which he converted two years later into his heroic poem of 'Charlie Cain, the cox'.

> And the thunder of the rocks,...
> And the fury and the din,
> And the horror and the roar,
> Rolling in, rolling in,
> Rolling in upon the dead lee-shore!

In April, 1890, he stayed at Port Erin (which he always called Port Iern according to the old Manx pronunciation) and while on a yachting expedition from that Port heard from the lips of Bob Lucas, one of the crew—a man devoted to him and generally regarded as the prototype of 'Tom Baynes'—the story of 'Jus' the shy', upon which he built the first number in the series entitled *In the Coach*.

In June of this year he was saddened by his friend Wilson's resignation of the Headmastership of Clifton to become Vicar of Rochdale and Archdeacon of Manchester. Under his successor, the Rev. M. G. Glazebrook, Brown worked loyally on: but with a relaxed cheerfulness in his work, which by this time was evidently impairing his health.

In June, 1891, he heard of the death of his only surviving brother, Will, whom he had not seen for forty years. Of the children brought up at Braddan Vicarage, Tom and his sister Margaret were now the only ones surviving, and to her he wrote, 'We must now expect our own summons. The other side is filling, and if it were not for my children I should feel my place over there rather than here'. From his vacation-lodgings at Keswick in September he crossed to the Island with Mr Hall Caine for a week-end, and on the Sunday evening took his companion to Kirk Maughold Church, and knelt at the altar place where he had been married thirty-four years before (Hall Caine, a little child, was playing in the road as the wedding party went by). Maughold Churchyard held the small grave of his first-born, Anny, the 'Bud so rare' of *Epistola ad Dakyns*.

In January, 1892, an attack of influenza shattered his nervous system terribly; and even when a sunny April helped his recovery, a load of depression lay heavily on him. 'I believe it is all up with me'; he wrote to a friend, 'I may go on for a few years more, but the mainspring has been rudely shaken.' After a fortnight at Preston, he moved to Hazlemere and spent a happy three weeks with Mr and Mrs Dakyns. But he had decided to give up his House and Mastership. On July the 2nd he closed his lecture books and T. E. B.'s career as a Schoolmaster was at an end. His daughters had gone ahead of him to prepare the new little house in Windsor Mount (No. 10), Ramsey. While they were thus occupied he went to London and had his portrait painted for the College by Sir William Richmond (it hangs in the Library); thence to stay with his old colleague Worthington at Devonport for a few days; and from Devonport he travelled alone to Liverpool, and next day to the Isle of Man, henceforth to be his home.

VI

(i)

Look on me, sun, ere thou set
   In the far sea;
From the gold and the rose and the jet
   Look full at me!
Leave on my brow a trace
   Of tenderest light;
Kiss me upon the face,
   Kiss for Good-night.

(ii)

'Weary wind of the West
   Over the billowy sea—
Come to my heart, and rest!
   Ah, rest with me!
Come from the distance dim
   Bearing the sun's last sigh;
I hear thee sobbing for him
   Through all the sky.'

So the wind came,
   Purpling the middle sea,
Crisping the ripples of flame—
   Came unto me;
Came with a rush to the shore,
   Came with a bound to the hill,
Fell, and died at my feet—
   Then all was still.

Since this Memoir is intended primarily for Manxmen, and to celebrate on May the 5th, 1930, the centenary of Brown's birth, a page
or two must be devoted to the few years of his retirement upon the

Island, little as they contained of incident, although strenuous enough whenever health permitted. The Island welcomed him back most hospitably, and he renewed many old friendships, receiving constant visits from Hall Caine, Mr Quine, Mr Rydings, Mr Frederick Lamothe, Mr and Mrs Arthur Moore, and beginning new but lasting friendships with Mrs Graves and her family at Peel, Dr and Mrs Wood at Douglas, and many others. At first he thoroughly enjoyed his leisure—reading, writing, playing and singing—for he lived within a few yards of the sea, 'the great challenger and promoter of song'.

The mornings would see him walking on the sea shore for three hours at a stretch by the water's edge, or along the brows overlooking Ramsey Bay; and in these walks he composed those lyrics which, welcomed by W. E. Henley for *The National Observer*, probably did more for his fame than all his earlier Manx poems. The rest of the day would be spent in writing these down, in miscellaneous reading, and in penning those letters to his intimate friends which fill the second volume of Mr Irwin's collection.

This was the routine, and he kept to it in the face of the autumn gales. But already, early in September, he had been up North Barrule; and when spring came, after a winter of heavy gales, he was

Off to the meadows, the meadows again!

To S. T. IRWIN

Baldrine, Lonan, Isle of Man

21 *May* 1893

I have come here to the house of my brother-in-law for a week. Ramsey is occupied by three regiments of volunteers from the adjacent Isle.

I walked over the mountains yesterday, and finished in a labyrinth of lovely glens, imperfectly known by me. The sweetest of solitudes, each one. It is so delicious to pore over a country like this, and draw out the very soul of it. As I descended I caught sight of three great steamers advancing towards the coast. I laughed and rejoiced greatly....

You will gather that I am much improved in health. My walk yesterday was a good twelve miles across mountains. I plucked some bell-heather nicely in flower; very early, is it not? Most exquisitely lovely the walk was! Not a soul for four hours; then converse with a good old soul, who was preparing a field for planting; the happy *agricola* who, having sailed all over the world, really does know 'his own goods'. We talked of the past, the Island past, so simple of analysis for both of us. The succession of farmers, the succession of parsons, till we got back to 'that's the man that christened me'. Then we stopped and looked into each other's eyes. The cuckoo called, and down the vale I went with no vacillating step....

I found a foxglove fairly out: that, too, was early. The mountains had the midsummer smell—a wonderful concoction; the glens perplexed me with an even more subtle aroma. Upon smells it is hard to reflect, so that I have not yet determined what it was. The glens were very full of blue-bells, and the flower of the mountain-ash, but I don't think I have got it; no. Some divine footsteps— what? Ah, sweet thing! was it you? In such valleys the sons of God might not unfitly wander, and find not a few daughters of men meet for the ineffable embrace. At any rate, heaven itself walked down the valley and lingered there, 'and deludhed me ter'ble'.

But very soon a hundred activities began to encroach on his leisure and holiday keeping. Various parishes desired Sermons from him, and he gave them generously. He gave public lectures at Ramsey, Peel, Douglas; whole series of them on 'Manx Character', 'The Manx Mountains', 'Old Kirk Braddan', 'Manx Poets', 'Manx Idioms'. He conducted farewell services for the Peel fleet prior to the Kinsale fishing, services when the fleets returned, services at his old School. He became a stout public defender of rights-of-way, especially that along the cliffs from Peel Hill to Glen Meay, 'trespassing' boldly wherever he scented a threat to a footpath,

4-2

thrusting past what he described as 'Redans, Malakoffs, Demilunes, Mamelons—the horrid, horrent diabolically perverse impediments', and defying prosecution. A box of manuscripts was lent him by his friend A. W. Moore, containing over five hundred eighteenth-century letters. These he studied in preparation for a projected work, *The Island Diocese*; which, however, never came to publication.

Some of these activities naturally exposed him to criticism. Some few of his countrymen, for example, resented a passage or two in his lecture on 'The Manx Character'. Brown claimed to have spoken the truth. He was not an advocate (he said) but a judge; he did *not* think lodging-house-keeping an occupation for young Manxmen. In the Colonies they did splendidly, and he held that, failing opportunities for manly work at home, a knowledge of emigration fields should be given in the Schools. His brother, Hugh, had gone out into the world and applied a harder, alien judgment. Thomas could not censure so. His own final verdict was that though the Manxman had faults such as proneness to exaggeration, fondness for gossip, vagueness of statement, trad-dy-liooar ('time enough'), imitation of trippers and lack of initiative, these faults were outweighed by sterling qualities such as sobriety, frugality, skill, industry, shrewdness: and on the whole he was 'good and sound and a man to live with'. The bulk of the Islanders realised that in this great countryman restored to them they had a priceless possession.

At the end of 1894 he was again offered the Archdeaconry of the Island, but declined on the ground that he wished to be free to do what he liked, say what he liked, write what he liked, within the limits prescribed by his own sense of what was seemly and fitting. And these pages will have missed their aim if they have failed to present Brown as actuated throughout life by a humble sense of service (but see for this the magnificent conclusion of his *Homini* Δημιουργός) combined with a passionate urge—insular, yet not narrow—to concentrate this service upon the core; craving only, in return for it, continuity; to live somehow somewhere after death and be remembered—

> I would not be forgotten in this land.

This craving for continuity, be it observed, was pure and unselfish. By a fallacy of thought, perhaps, but by a very noble one, he transferred the ambition to those for whom he laboured. His own terror that Time might obliterate the moment,

> And all this personal dream be fled,

became for his countrymen a very spring of helpfulness. *Antiquam exquirite matrem*—he would do that which they, in poverty, and the stress of earning daily bread, were careless to do—would explore for them the ancient springs of faith and custom.

> Dear countrymen, whate'er is left to us
>> Of ancient heritage—
>> Of manners, speech, of humours, polity,
>> The limited horizon of our stage—
>> Old love, hope, fear,
>> All this I fain would fix upon the page;
>> That so the coming age,
>> Lost in the empire's mass,
>> Yet haply longing for their fathers, here
>> May see, as in a glass,
>> What they held dear—
> May say, ''Twas thus and thus
>> They lived'; and as the time-flood onward rolls
>> Secure an anchor for their Keltic souls.

His own philosophy on this subject, so poignantly vital to him, may be gathered from the two following extracts, the one personal, the other general. The first is addressed to his sister Margaret, discussing the possibility of a Memoir of his brother Hugh:

Ramsey

25 *November* 1894

I have sometimes a misgiving that we Browns make too much of ourselves. But we were, the more I think of it, an extraordinary family; and who is to know it if you and I, the only survivors, do not exclaim it to the world? (!) And the world will laugh at us? D—it! let them; i.e. the contemporary world. But I would leave it with the utmost confidence to the future. I know what the future will think of the present, how it will stand affected to our generation. Depend upon it, the last word has not been said. A book of that sort, utterly neglected at the time it was published, would lie as dead as ... a chrysalis; but it would have its day; wings would lie hidden in the brittle case, and the light of a cleaner air would be for it to pierce through and permeate. But a chrysalis? A butterfly? An ephemeran? Poor book! One thing is certain that I would give worlds for just such a book disinterred from the dustheap of, say, the 17th century. And is not this a natural feeling, one that we can calculate on?

The second and more general one was addressed—

To MISS GRAVES

Ramsey

15 *June* 1897

... You say you don't believe in a future state, but you have 'gleams of hope'. We are all much in the same plight. So was old Jowett, you remember. Implicit believers in the Bible are all right. Independently of revelation, the matter is a question of metaphysics, and a very subtle one. It has beset humanity from the very beginning, and (this is important) you can't lay the ghost. Rest for a moment from the pressing concerns of the present life, and there you are, you and your question. It is the inevitable attitude of the soul, what one might call its obvious native polarity. 'The gleams' are blessed things, just caught at our noblest throbs and in our most ecstatic moods. That they are ecstatic, as apprehended by us, does not disprove their essential permanence. Rather it suggests the contrary. Metaphysically the balance is in favour of a future state.

To a sceptical nature like mine, the *balance* is everything. That is what I get from my own reflections, or rather, what I got ages ago, helped by Plato, confirmed by Butler. It was done once for all; you can't re-open these metaphysical problems. Let sleeping dogs lie. I invite no one to go back into them with me. To those who have no aptness for metaphysical speculations I would say, 'Stop where you are! Accept the opinion of the majority. The greatest thinkers of all ages have believed in the future state. They have thought it out for you: be content. In a hundred difficult matters you act upon similar testimony'. Rest assured it is not *persons*, and such folk, that have passed through the region of shadows into the light of the eternal day; no, but the great fixed stars of the human race, pondering, reflecting, judicious. If, at the end of their great communings, somewhat of a rapture of intoxication has seized them, what wonder? They have seen the King in His beauty. Give them credit for honesty, for intelligence, for a sympathy with human wants, for absolute fairness, for burning love. That is how I think of them and feel towards them. With tottering steps I have accompanied them. But that was years ago. Now I don't want to totter, but to walk steadily. Therefore, I say, unhesitatingly, 'I believe'.

As for continuity in human remembrance—I confess that, in going through the poems and letters for the purpose of this Memoir, I have found myself constantly haunted by the lines of another poet—Hood's noble sonnet on *Death*:

It is not death, that sometime in a sigh
This eloquent breath shall take its speechless flight;
That sometime these bright stars, that now reply
In sunlight to the sun, shall set in night;
That this warm conscious flesh shall perish quite,
And all life's ruddy springs forget to flow;
That thoughts shall cease, and the immortal sprite
Be lapp'd in alien clay and laid below;
It is not death to know this,—but to know
That pious thoughts, which visit at new graves
In tender pilgrimage, will cease to go
So duly and so oft,—and when grass waves
Over the past-away, there may be then
No resurrection in the minds of men.

'Diuturnity', says Brown's seventeenth-century namesake, 'is a dream and folly of expectation. There is nothing strictly immortal but immortality.'

But at least in these last years on the Island he realised his temporal dream, and it did not disappoint him. He could not, indeed, carry off his old friends to share it, but he could return to England and visit them or stay at home and write to them concerning the realisation, and be sure they understood: for not even Brown could tear himself back to boyhood from age, unthreading the ties of his middle years. The Island society, revisited, was dear, but could not supply the full need (unconsciously acquired) for intellectual converse. He had to fill a great part of the day with correspondence. The mass of his letters belongs to this period. They continue cheerful to the end, though they disclose him as increasingly aware that the end was in sight, even near.

In November, returning from one of these visits to England, he had a wretched passage of twelve hours from Liverpool to Ramsey, and arrived home far from well.

9 November 1896

At Liverpool my practised eye detected the symptoms of a storm outside. And a storm we had! A twopenny-halfpenny miscreant of a little steamer crawled shamefaced up to the stage. I never saw anything under steam or canvas more disreputable. She seemed to apologize for her very existence, and is, though so small, a notorious 'rowler'. So 'we rowled, and we rowled, and we rowled'. I, of course, went below, and availed myself of my ancient seamanship to remain there. But, what with sea-sick women and children who will persist in overflowing into what we used to call the 'gentlemen's cabin', I had a hard time of it; much alleviated, though, by Fitz,[1] whom I read as long as daylight lasted. The wind had risen and pursued us, and just in the nick of time turned with a vicious twist into the north-east, making it impossible to land at the Long Pier. So we had to wait till high water at eleven lying-to in the bay, 'rowling' gunwales under, and smashing the crockery at an infernal

---

1 I.e. *The Letters of Edward Fitz Gerald.*

rate. The captain came down to tell me how matters stood, or 'rowled', or jumped, or generally played old Harry....

I landed in the teeth of a fierce north-easter—nice work for a man recent from bedroom fires and hot grog! When I got up to my house, my people were all snug between the blankets. I knocked them up, and what may come I know not.

What followed was a severe cold, alleviated by writing at an article on Spenser for the *New Review*, edited by Sir Henry Newbolt; by his books; and notably by a first reading of Stevenson's *Weir of Hermiston*, which he proclaimed a masterpiece. 'If the Century runs out upon this final chord, what more do I want? Let me die with the sough of it in my ears.'

T. E. Brown left the Island for the last time on October the 1st, 1897. He first stayed with his old colleague Wollaston at Clifton for ten days, and then withdrew to Cardiff, where he spent another ten days with his sister and her husband, the Rev. J. Williamson. She noticed that he was not his usual self, although his mind was as bright as ever. Several evenings were spent reading through his letters to his mother and sister (the earliest of which had been written fifty years before), making comments, pointing out what might be preserved and what destroyed, and finally committing the whole collection to the Williamsons.

On the 25th he returned to Clifton, and on the 27th attended a Richter Concert with two of his old colleagues, Wollaston and Tait, with the latter of whom he was staying. The next evening, says Mr Irwin, 'he dined with me and seemed his usual bright self, and read one of his poems at my sister's request, but did not finish it, saying he was tired'.

On Friday evening, the 29th, he gave an address to the boys of his old House on 'The Ideals of Clifton'. He spoke for some minutes with great vigour: then suddenly his voice grew thick, and he was seen to stagger. He died in less than two hours.

He was buried beside his wife in the Churchyard of Redland

Chapel, across the Downs. A white marble cross on the grave bears the following inscription:

Rev: Thomas Brown died Oct. 29th 1897. Keep thy heart with all diligence, for out of it are the issues of life.

Other inscriptions perpetuate the memory of Amelia Brown, his wife, who died July 3rd, 1888, aged 57; Braddan Brown, their child, who died April 21st, 1876, aged 7; and Thomas Birkett Brown, their son, who died July 5th, 1919.

Hugh, the youngest son of T. E. Brown, died in New Zealand in October, 1921.

VII

The sum of happiness in the world is not too large. I would like, if possible, to increase it by the modest contribution of my own store. If so, I must guard it from all disturbance; and poetry enables me to do this, gives me a thousand springs of joy, in none of which there is one drop of bitterness—and thank God for that!

Letter to G. QUARRY, *Jan.* 20, 1885.

In 'placing' Brown as a poet among his contemporaries it is difficult to sift out judgment from personal affection—the more difficult again because he was so unlike them all, *sui generis*, and yet originated no 'school'. Nor is it easy to predict his permanence; his isolation being (if the reader will pass the phrase) so deliberately insular. For some seventy-five *per centum* of his verse—for all his longer poems— he used the Manx dialect: and although every page can be easily read—although he avoided William Barnes's mistake of making true poetry repellent by printing it in symbols of phonetic—it takes a genius at least as eminent as Burns's to lift dialect to the level of the *eloquium vulgare*, the accepted language of English Poetry. But let us leave this question for the moment with Brown himself. In a familiar letter[1] he asks—

Did you ever try to write a Burns song? I mean, the equivalent in ordinary English of his Scotch? Can it be done? A Yorkshireman —could he do it? A Lancashire man (Waugh)? I hardly think so. The Ayrshire dialect has a *Schwung* and a confidence that no English county can pretend to. Our dialects are apologetic things, half-ashamed, half-insolent. Burns has no doubts: or has his dialect taken this position just because it was *his*?

We postpone the question and answer; because after all, dialect and degrees of skill in handling it belong to technique, not to the core of the matter—as Brown again recognised, and taught in his lines on *Poets and Poets*—

> He fishes in the night of deep sea pools:
>   For him the nets hang long and low,
> Cork-buoyed and strong; the silver-gleaming schools
>   Come with the ebb and flow
> Of universal tides, and all the channels glow.
>
> Or, holding with his hand the weighted line,
>   He sounds the languor of the neaps;
> Or feels what current of the springing brine
>   The cord divergent sweeps,
> The throb of what great heart bestirs the middle deeps.
>
> Thou also weavest meshes, fine and thin,
>   And leaguer'st all the forest ways;
> But of that sea and the great heart therein
>   Thou knowest nought: whole days
> Thou toil'st, and hast thy end—good store of pies and jays.

So let us follow the devil's advocate when he would get to the vital gap in the armour and strike at it: for which he has a very sharp (and fair) weapon in Brown's own confession to being 'a born

1 To J. C. Tarver, February the 18th, 1894.

sobber'. The fellow can go on to argue, with a plenty of useful evidence, that here was a man who wore his heart upon his sleeve, inviting the daws: and the charge would seem to lie, even when we have sifted out the fair from the unfair evidence, of which more than enough has been published by well-intentioned friends. Brown was a passionate man, and reacted most passionately to the two greatest sorrows of his life, which yet are sorrows incident to all men—the loss of a loved child at the age of seven and, later, the loss of his wife. But even sternly self-disciplined men give way to wild, incoherent outbursts on the first incidence of such blows, especially in letters to intimate friends; to be corrected afterwards, by whatsoever religion or philosophy the sufferer recovers acceptance, sanity, and is himself again. Wherefore the publication of the quick violent outcries in private letters seems to me to weight the charge unfairly, with so much evidence to hand, in other letters, of second thoughts, manly resignation, equipoise. Nevertheless we have to grant that a poet gives himself up to be judged by what he deliberately publishes; for these *are* his second thoughts and he invites us to share them. And here the devil's advocate is on firm ground, calling our attention, for instance, to this in *Clevedon Verses*:

> She knelt upon her brother's grave,
> 　　My little girl of six years old—
> He used to be so good and brave,
> 　　The sweetest lamb of all our fold;
> He used to shout, he used to sing,
> Of all our tribe the little king—
> And so unto the turf her ear she laid,
> To hark if still in that dark place he played.
> No sound! no sound!
> Death's silence was profound;
> And horror crept
> Into her aching heart, and Dora wept.
> If this is as it ought to be,
> My God, I leave it unto Thee.

An even more absolute prostration of grief, in the same place and for the same cause, may be found in a passage of Brown's *Letters* by those who care to intrude upon it. But that was a confession for private eyes: *this* is written in verse and printed, implying a two-fold deliberation: and its deliberateness invites the question, 'If *this* be all its conclusion, of what use is the lyric to anyone save to the poet as a discharge of his own emotion?' It may be a *catharsis* giving him personal relief: but if it excite in the reader no more than luxury in some remembered woe of his own, offering no solace or companionable help, why publish it? The present writer, of his own experience—of his own observation, too often claimed, during the sorrowful years 1914–18—as of his colder detached study confirming both—has argued elsewhere that men and women in extremity of bereavement do not write elegies at all: that they are dumb as Niobe; even tears coming through agony of relief.

> I tell you hopeless grief is passionless;
>   That only men incredulous of despair,
>   Half-taught in anguish, through the midnight air
> Beat upward to God's throne in loud access
> Of shrieking and reproach....

This, however, raises a question or rather many questions concerning the comparative genuineness of personal sorrow and any reflex of it in deliberate verse—too deep for discussion here, or at any rate tempting to speculations that might seem to interrupt this Memoir by irrelevance. Indeed the subject is dangerous; and, pathos lying so near in practice to humour, is the quaggy edge of temptation into a treatise. And in such a treatise one would probably have to divide the claims of (say) first love and mature grief to deliver themselves without restraint.

So let it be enough to say that Brown as a 'sobber' was not afraid of letting himself go, whether in exposing his own emotions or in depicting those of others. Consider the extreme anguish he expresses in *Mater Dolorosa* from the 'greeting' of any mother over any dead child—

> Aw, Billy, good sowl! don't cuss! don't cuss!
> Ye see, these angels is grand to nuss;
> And it's lek they're feedin' them on some nice air,
> Or dew or the lek, that's handy there—
> O Billy, look at my poor bress!...
>   And...O my head!
> Billy, Billy, come to bed!...
> And the little things that navar knew sin—
> And everything as nate as a pin...:
> But won't he want me when he'll be wakin'?
> Will they take him up when he's wantin' takin'?
> I hope he'll not be left in the dark—
> He was allis used to make a wark
> If a body 'd lave him the smallest minute—
> Dear me! the little linnet—
> But I forgot—it's allis light
> In yandhar place...All right! all right!...
>   *Light* was I sayin'? but who can tell?
> Bad for the eyes, though...but a little curtain
> On a string, ye know—aw certain! certain!
> Let me feel your face, Billy! Jus' us two!
> Aw, Billy, the sorry I am for you!...

...until a sensitive hand can hardly go on copying it down. 'Abuse of pathos', says the devil's advocate. 'Yes...pathos at any rate pushed to extreme', the careful critic agrees. And yet...can we separate an indulgence in pathos from that gift of humour which we prize as something rather particular in our literature? Chaucer was not afraid of pathos in combination with humour, nor even Shakespeare in ending Falstaff, nor Swift in his Letters, nor Sterne certainly; nor Goldsmith, nor Cowper, nor Scott—and, above all for confident use of it, not Dickens. Now these were all great men of their hands.

Without any comparison of size, Brown was of these men's breed and quality—of their 'stuff'. Even in size of *understanding* he could match himself with them—as he could match himself with Burns in the sense that Burns, for all the multitude of his idolators, has probably never struck a chord more accurately responsive in echo than he struck into the vitals of Brown: and Burns, Heaven knows, can be pathetic until the kye come hame.

And so—for the last count in the indictment—his free indulgence in mirth alongside of his tears has laid our man open to the charge or insinuation that he was, or could be, at times something of a buffoon.

And here at last we get the devil's advocate choked by a long rope in his own stupidity. For Brown himself was too large altogether to be careful of the impression he gave. He had his reserves, to be sure (as all true men have), and more of them than a casual or hasty reading of his Poems or his Letters would suggest—more of them, one fears, than this Memoir has managed to convey. Actually, in daily life or toward strangers, his habitual bearing would be somewhat donnish, aloof, with more than a touch of old-mannered courtesy. But in congenial company or correspondence with his friends (and it must be remembered that almost all the letters preserved to us are written to dear and understanding friends) he would let himself go, just as in company with such intimates he would strip himself naked for a swim and, emerging, kick himself on beach or bank in the pure riot of living. Further it must be remembered that he was partly a Scot of the Burns type by descent; and some readers will hardly need to be told that the Scot, formal in converse, is apt (unlike an Englishman) to cast away reserve when he takes pen in hand—to be far more confidential, more expansive, than allowed by what Homer would call 'the barrier of the teeth'. In any company that encouraged him it must be allowed that Brown, like many another over-shy man, would break bounds. As he confesses in a letter to Irwin[1]—and the confession may be taken as one of many—

My lecture in Douglas on 'Old Kirk Braddan' was a failure. The

---

[1] January the 29th, 1895.

people were most hearty and indulgent; so it must have been my
own fault. Portraits of my father, and my brother Hugh, were
botched and feeble. You will not see them. The fact is the people
were too indulgent, stimulated me to unstinted mimicry—buffoonery
—what you will. And they laughed and laughed, till with horror
I awoke to the consciousness that I was treating the old Braddan life
as a School of Comedy, of which my father constituted the chief
figure and protagonist. Some tender things I believe I said; but the
subjective condition of my hearers, aggravated by my own impu-
dence, carried everything away into a βάραθρον of farce. Vae mihi!

'The subjective condition of my hearers'—at once the encourage-
ment and the trap of Keltic rhetoric! Add to it the Kelt's up-and-
down of emotion, his super-sensitiveness to the next morning's
headache; add again the life-long lesson which Oxford had con-
strained upon a young Islander's self-consciousness; and we may
divine with what undue pain, even in late life, these lapses, these
releases from the 'rigid irony' which he carried as his armour—and
his burden—tormented him.

But it seems to me that altogether too much has been squeezed by
critics out of Brown's personal confessions—the confessions of a
modestly minded man avid of sympathy—to intimate friends in
letters never intended for publication. The plain business, accepted
by me, of writing a Memoir is to reveal the man as closely as
sympathy can do it and delicacy permits. But, in the end, Brown will
have to be judged by what he deliberately published of himself to
the world, and not what he chose to impart to his intimates. He
must, by all but the thinning number of those who knew him, be
reckoned eminent or useful, or less than either, by his Poetry, as
by that he must be finally ranked. The pages of this volume
attempt to recapture, to marshal, impressions and memories of him
through his transient years. But to those who never knew him he
must be *aut poeta aut nullus*: and Poetry remains, after all definitions
made of it, *the actual matter that poets have written.*
Now if we simply consider what Brown slowly and deliberately

yielded of himself to the public, we shall discover little in it of the mere 'sobber', and nothing at all of the 'buffoon'. In the matter of laughter he holds the wise universal note. Witness his *Risus Dei*:

Methinks in Him there dwells alway
A sea of laughter very deep,
Where the leviathans leap,
And little children play,
Their white feet twinkling on its crisped edge;
But in the outer bay
The strong man drives the wedge
Of polished limbs,
And swims.
Yet there is one will say—
'It is but shallow, neither is it broad'.
And so he frowns; but is he nearer God?...

Nay, 'tis a Godlike function; laugh thy fill!
Mirth comes to thee unsought;
Mirth sweeps before it like a flood the mill
Of languaged logic; thought
Hath not its source so high;
The will
Must let it by:
For though the heavens are still,
God sits upon His hill,
And sees the shadows fly;
And if He laughs at fools, why should He not?

Indeed—if one may speculate idly on things that might once have been and now never can be—I could pray that fate, reversing its wheel, had permitted Brown to pour out all the lyric that must have sung within him in early youth. We—or, let me say, others of later time who knew him not—could then have sifted out gold from rubbish. But how much of treasurable gold we have lost through accident or the circumstances of his life let anyone consider who, reading *Fo'c's'le Yarns*, finds himself aware of the incessant lyrical urge in them, and then goes on to reflect that almost all the songs into which Brown put his heart were written in middle age or toward its close.

That, as it seems to me, is the key to him. Repressed in youth; engaged to work for his 'classes' at Oxford; afterwards engaged at Clifton on the daily round, the common task; he found his release too late. Or shall we say that he discovered his release in mature years when ordinary men, having missed in youth to strike the full gush from the rock, find that

The mount is mute, the channel dry?

It certainly was so with Brown: and it certainly is not for a lover of his poems to vex himself with a question such as he might use over a bin of claret—'It is full-bodied, of appreciable soil. But the trouble is that its vinosity and fragrance seem uncannily mature. Will it keep?'

Well, I for one feel very sure that T. E. B.'s vintage is going, at any rate, to 'keep': even as, to speak of other cellars, the wines of Landor and Peacock will keep, being true juice of the Muses' grapes; and by the truthfulness of that juice he will come to be estimated long after this generation has gone its ways.

But the point to be emphasised here—and I reserve a later one equally important—is that the bulk of his poetry is Manx, and truly Manx: of a piece with English literature as (let me say) Henryson's *Testament of Cresseid* is of a piece with it, but native and Manx nevertheless. For my own part—given the tales he wanted to tell— I can conceive no happier medium of verse than that which he invented. While smacking nothing of the scholar, it just uses (as Chaucer did) whatever advantage comes to hand: and the result, as with Chaucer, is something genuine, *a per se*. On this matter of *genuineness* in poetry Mr Selwyn Simpson[1] has saved me trouble by drawing deadly parallels—Brown's untrussed dialect set under Tennyson's artifice in words:

1 *Thomas Edward Brown, the Manx Poet*, by Selwyn G. Simpson, 1906.

Enoch Arden
    A narrow cave ran in beneath the cliff;
    In this the children play'd at keeping house.
    Enoch was host one day, Philip the next,
    While Annie still was mistress; but at times
    Enoch would hold possession for a week:
    'This is my house, and this my little wife!'
    'Mine too', said Philip; 'turn and turn about':
    When if they quarrell'd Enoch stronger-made
    Was master: then would Philip, his blue eyes
    All flooded with the helpless wrath of tears,
    Shriek out 'I hate you, Enoch!' and at this
    The little wife would weep for company.

Betsy Lee
    Now the beauty of the thing when childher plays is
    The terrible wonderful length the days is.
    Up you jumps, and out in the sun,
    And you fancy the day will never be done;
    And you're chasin' the bumbees hummin' so cross
    In the hot sweet air among the goss [gorse],
    Or gath'rin' bluebells or lookin' for eggs,
    Or peltin' the ducks with their yalla legs,
    Or a-climbin' and nearly breakin' your skulls,
    Or a-shoutin' for divilment after the gulls,
    Or a thinkin' of nothin', but down at the tide
    Singin' out for the happy you feel inside.

Or take again—of First Love in its approach—

Enoch Arden
    But when the dawn of rosy childhood past,
    And the new warmth of life's ascending sun
    Was felt by either, either fixt his heart
    On that one girl.

Betsy Lee
    Ah, mates! it's wonderful too—the years
    You may live dead-on-end with your eyes and your ears
    Right alongside the lass that's goin'
    To be your sweetheart, and you never knowin'.

Upon these appositions I will only say that Brown did this particular thing better than Tennyson, because more naturally: as I shall add but a word, and that on a matter of technique, to the full and sympathetic discussion of the *Fo'c's'le Yarns* with which Mr Costain has graced some later pages of our volume. It seems to me that few, even among Brown's sworn admirers, have ever quite realised how perfect a vehicle, metrically, he invented—for it was invention—for these homely tales. If one may say it and escape suspicion of derogating from either, Brown's verse avoids alike the stiltedness, with the accompanying air of patronage, which now and again jars upon us in Crabbe, and the pedantic rusticity—pedantic mainly through obtrusive spelling, but pedantic none the less and, because pedantic, felt as patronising—which interferes between us and full enjoyment of William Barnes's lovely Eclogues. Brown's chosen metre is so flexible to his purpose always; and whether that purpose be tragic or comic or sentimental, lending itself to command of rhyme and matter; that it apparently flows of pure instinct: the tale simply 'runs on', just telling itself. What higher praise, when one comes to think of it, can be given?...And, as for the sentiment,—We have all fallen into a fashion, nowadays, of sneering at sentiment and confusing it with sentimentality—a word which should be used only of affected or false sentiment. What is the matter with sentiment, if only it be true? What wrong, for a particular instance, with *Ye banks and braes o' bonnie Doon*? Or, for a general one, what foolish, what unnatural in the moisture of an exile's eyes over a plant received from home—in any 'home thought from abroad'? True sentiment is, as Brown practised and would have preached, a thing as universal as true laughter.

But—and it connects with this—the reader had, in a line or two quoted just now, a hint of Brown's reverential, almost sacramental attitude towards First Love. (It held something of the humorous too: but so did his attitude towards many things sacred to him—as a perfect lover will tease his beloved now and then, because they both are of the sanctuary, and understand.) Yet it leads to a sad speculation. Circumstances, and the urge to study much in order that he might earn a living and help his family, repressed the poet in him during his youth. His poetical faculty developed late, as this Memoir has told; his *lyrical* faculty (to my thinking the acme of that gift in him), later yet. What priceless passionate songs have we not lost through that accident of fate?

An idle speculation? Yes, of course: but who can read *Roman Women*—that 'amazing' composition, as Sir Francis Newbolt truly calls it—without speculating on the *maturity* of Brown's flowering time (in itself a miracle): without asking himself 'If such a thing could be done of the dry wood, what might not have come of the green?'

> Close by the Mamertine
> Her eyes swooped into mine,
> O Jove supreme!
> What gleam
> Of sovereignty! what hate—
> Large, disproportionate!
> What lust
> August!
> Imperial state
> Of full-orbed throbbings solved
> In vast and dissolute content—
> Love-gluts revolved
> In lazy rumination, rent,
> As then, by urgence of the immediate sting!
> The tiger spring
> Is there; the naked strife
> Of sinewy gladiators, knife
> Slant urged....

And this potency of passion delayed its full power to wait on maturity, acceptance, resignation!—

> I ask one prayer,
> The which, if it be granted,
> It skills not where
> Thou plantest me, only I would be planted...

—and in lyrics sub-sorrowful, wise—

> To live within a cave—it is most good.
>   But, if God make a day,
>   And some one come and say,—
> 'Lo! I have gathered faggots in the wood!'
>   E'en let him stay,
> And light a fire and fan a temporal mood!
>
> So sit till morning! When the light is grown
>   That he the path can read;
>   Then bid the man God-speed!
> His morning is not thine: yet must thou own
> They have a cheerful warmth—those ashes on the stone.

One more necessary thing must, I think, be observed of Brown. He belonged to his period and to what we may call the tradition of Clough (his predecessor of the Oriel time): and that period was preoccupied with intellectual doubt, religious questioning, a general *malaise* which, as with Clough, inhibited free utterance: and we can only get, perhaps, at its secret when we arrive at its threnody in Matthew Arnold's *Thyrsis*. Reading that, we can understand. Now, if one mistake not, Brown, in spite of filial ties and the pull of old remembrance, never surrendered himself wholly to the Church of his fathers. His hesitancy in proceeding to Priest's Orders, his twice refusing to be made Archdeacon would indicate this, even did his poems not prove it. In short he was born a Pantheist (with something of the Pagan, even the Faun, in him) and indulged throughout life his natural sense of God inhering in all things—in the sea, for example, in the poor folk plying their trade on it, in the very fish they took—

>   from Ocean's gate
>   Keen for the foaming spate
>   The true God rushes in the salmon.

It was for him a God (as we can read in the conclusion of *Dartmoor Verses*) not necessarily, or even probably, Omnipotent; liable to make mistakes, as all grand artists are, but all the more lovable for that; not a static Creator (for who, interrogating what he feels to be the best in him, or in the things he once aspired to do and once imagined himself capable of doing, can conceive of a static Creator creating Man in His image?), but a Creator sedulous to improve through love of His creature: not Omnipotent but Omnipresent even by the humblest of hearths; most comprehensible always, most near to be held, in the glens of His worshipper's most dear Island: the inhabitants of which on the hundredth anniversary of this poet's birth praise him now, as is just.

ARTHUR QUILLER-COUCH

APPENDIX

Personal Recollections and Impressions

BY

VARIOUS FRIENDS

I

MEMORIES OF T. E. BROWN

by

J. M. WILSON, D.D.

LATE CANON AND LIBRARIAN OF WORCESTER,
FORMERLY OF ROCHDALE AND ARCHDEACON OF
MANCHESTER, AND SOMETIME HEADMASTER
OF CLIFTON COLLEGE

MY DEAR ATTORNEY-GENERAL:

I am very glad to hear that the Isle of Man is going to celebrate Brown's centenary; and as it is possible, even probable, that I am the only man surviving who can remember Brown at school for a few weeks only in the autumn of the year 1848 and spring of 1849, I feel I must contribute a few memories of him.

I was then a little lad of nearly twelve and he was more than eighteen, and he was on the point of leaving for Oxford. I remember him perfectly; and my looking on him with awe as he appeared at 'the break', standing, talking with his friends, laughing, joking joyously, for the few minutes of open air. A square, erect, sturdy figure, grave generally but exploding into laughter; always the centre of a group of two or three of his companions. I remember someone telling me that he was 'a great swell'. It was reputed that he knew more than any master; and was said to have written the best Latin prose that the University examiners had ever seen. F. W. Farrar had just left the school. T. Fowler was there still, and other giants at whom we looked with reverence. But Brown, we thought, was more than they. Wherever he was, there was life at its fullest. Of course, he never saw or spoke to a youngster like me.

He lived somewhere on The Green and walked up about half a mile to school. It was usually then that I saw him, coming to school or leaving it with his friends; but I remember the shouts of joyous laughter; the pause in the walk; the head thrown back; the grave listening, lips tight closed, the explosion into words, and the talk, endless, varied, brilliant.

This was during the half-year that his school days and mine overlapped. If I had never seen him again he would live as a distinct figure in my memory.

The next occasion on which I saw him was in the summer of 1853. I was then, along with my twin brother, head of the school, near the end of our seventeenth year. The school was in low water at that time, and very ineffective in its teaching. A great generation of boys had passed and left no successors. The school had fallen in numbers. Brown was there on the Speech Day, and 'took me up', and became my friend to the end of his days.

We, my brother and I, had been head of the school for a full year, and there was only one other boy in the first class with us, by name Ives, who went up in that year to St Catharine's, Cambridge—no scholar, but a lover of literature. When my brother and I left King William's College, we went to Sedbergh School in the summer of 1853 at nearly seventeen. We were examined by Evans, the first-rate Headmaster, and found to be backward and fragmentary in our attainments, and barely fit for the bottom of his first class of ten or twelve. Stimulus and scholarship had been alike wanting. Brown must have taught himself for two years at least. He and Farrar and Fowler, and one or two more, must have been at K. W. C. independent of any master.

In 1853 we won, of course, all the prizes at K. W. C. There was a Latin essay, Greek verse and Latin verse; and an English poem, won by excellent work by my brother (it was on the Duke of Wellington); Divinity Prizes; French Prizes; and others. I am inclined to tell the story of my winning the French Prize—a volume of Molière which still adorns my shelves. The French master (one Boully, if I recollect right) set the voluntary class who learnt French, on the last of his weekly visits, and on a half holiday, a piece of translation from *Télémaque*, and a piece of composition, and told us that the prize depended on our performance. The composition that in his laziness he set us was to turn the Ten Commandments into French! Arthur Griffiths (afterwards famous as the head of a great prison), who had lived for some time abroad and was known by us as 'Frenchy', was unquestionably far the best French scholar in the school. But he could not remember the Commandments! He appealed in vain for a Prayer Book. I knew them, and made some kind of translation of them and got the first prize for French! This was a specimen of the conduct of the school at that time. The standard was very low. It fills me with astonishment when I think over Brown's performances at ChristChurch and Oriel.

His memory was always fresh in the College. A year or two later, but before he came back as a master, I attended a prize day, and proposed cheers for some distinguished old members of the school. Major Anderson was present, who so gallantly defended Lucknow, and Captain Griffiths, my own senior contemporary, another hero of the Mutiny, wounded at the siege of Delhi. But I let myself go about Brown also; and the school showed that they had not forgotten him, and that he was among their demi-gods.

Do you know the story of Brown's *viva voce* in Greek translation before some of the College dons, at which old Gaisford, the Head, was present? Brown was set to translate at sight a scene in one of the plays of Aristophanes—I have forgotten which—between two non-Athenians, a Boeotian and some other dialect-speaking Greek. Brown was a splendid mimic, and translated one of the two into Irish, and the other into Scotch. The examiners were charmed. Gaisford stood by, in his usual solemn silence. At last he was heard to mutter in his deep voice, 'The young man construes well'. After a little he said out loud, 'The young man construes *very* well'. Still Brown was kept at it. At last Gaisford broke into a smile and exclaimed, 'The young man construes *exceedingly* well'.

Brown's career at Oxford, and his last triumph there, in winning an Oriel Fellowship, are too well known for me to relate.

My next meeting with Brown was when I was an undergraduate at St John's College, Cambridge, and spent part of a vacation on the Island. It was in 1857, I think. I stayed with Brown in his little lodgings at Derby Haven. We boated, and he was a master in seamanship. We raced off Fort Island in the early mornings, in a fresh breeze, the gunwale perilously near the water (as it seemed to me); trailing lines for fish and catching two or three; and then returning to breakfast. I cannot remember how long I stayed with him, but I remember one evening we spent at Van Laun's. He was then the French master, and lived on The Green. Van Laun met us at the door with a profound apology for his wife's absence. 'She was in Douglas', he explained, 'a most unfortunate engagement—she might return later.' This was said with the faintest possible wink to Brown, which he quite understood. The dinner was excellent; Mrs Van Laun came up from the kitchen in the evening, smiling and fresh! Brown and Van Laun—and I think Pleignier—were there; and the talk was indescribable.

During the following years Brown and I corresponded occasionally with one another; and when Percival was appointed to Clifton College, he asked me if I knew of someone to take the modern side. I named Brown; and Brown came over (to Rugby) to be interviewed. He spent an evening at my lodgings. About half a dozen of us dined there. I warned Brown that he must be on his good behaviour. He did not take my advice. Never was Brown so great. I still remember the Manx songs with their odd discordant pianoforte accompaniment and final shriek; the paradoxes; the torrent of fun and talk, and the stories—

> Stories, stories, nothing but stories,
> Spinnin' away to the height of your glories.

Percival, I think, was the first to leave, his usual gravity having been completely shattered. Next morning I asked him, not without anxiety, what he thought of Brown. 'Oh, he'll do', said Percival. And so he came to Clifton.

I have outlived my power of writing. But no description of Brown can be adequate. He was a combination of 'the Docthor' and 'the Pazon' of his poems.

> Lovin' is understandin'—eh?
> Lovin' is understandin'. Well,
> He'd a lovin' ould heart had Docthor Bell.

Brown, like 'the Docthor', understood all sorts of people because he loved them with a love—reverently be it spoken—like that with which we may imagine the Creator loves us all. That was the Doctor. And with that 'loving'—a love unknown to the merciless and frivolous, and to the self-righteous, he added the innocent gentleness of 'the Pazon'.

> True and kind; and the ebb and the flow
> Of all men's hearts went through and through him;
> The sweet ould man, if you'd only knew him.

I have known many men, great and small, in my long life; but I have never known a man so lovable, so great, so varied, so inspiring to one's understanding of men, so human, so truly wonderful, as T. E. Brown.

In the year 1914, I was invited to unveil the tablet erected on the garden wall of the house in Ramsey which was the last home of Brown, and in performing this most pleasant duty I attempted to estimate his genius. I cannot now do better than reproduce the substance of what I then said, as my address embodied my appreciation of some of his great qualities.

It is now nearly thirty years since Brown died, a period long enough for judges of literature, wherever English is spoken, to have realised his high and assured place in the temple of poetic fame.

Great writers found him out long ago. George Eliot wrote enthusiastically to Macmillan when *Betsy Lee* first appeared. Max
Müller, to whom with others, when staying at the Maloja Hotel in
1885 I read *The Doctor*, put it in his list of the hundred best books
of the world. He borrowed my copy, and read it to Browning at
Venice, and afterwards to the Empress Frederick at Berlin; and he
told me of their delight in it; and others known in the literary world
rank Brown among the Great Poets.

By this time Manxland has come to recognise by common consent
that he was her noblest son in brain and heart, and in sympathetic
insight into all that is most human and most divine. He gave the
last five years of his life to his Island home with lavish love. All his
varied knowledge and charm were at its service. Some still living
may remember his lectures—lectures unsurpassed in critical insight,
humour, and frank enjoyment. None who knew him will ever forget
the brilliancy and ease of his talk, his dramatic mimicry, his wide
literary knowledge, his vitalising critical judgment, his discriminating
love of music, and his ever fresh humour. He was the most delightful
of men, as acquaintance or friend. As someone said of him, 'You
never got to the end of Brown'. These personal reasons explain the
love and admiration of those who knew him; but the justification
for the centenary celebration must be sought elsewhere. It is in his
writings that he will live.

His claim for a permanent place in the ranks of literature rests on
his letters, his stories in verse or 'Yarns', mainly in the Anglo-Manx
dialect, and on his numerous lyrical and other short poems, in which
he reveals glimpses of his inmost soul, poems that are the fragmentary
expression of his life-long intimate communing with Nature and
with God.

Of his letters, unique as they are, I must leave it to others to speak.

But I must write a few words on his *Fo'c's'le Yarns*—his stories
of the life of Manx fisher-folk and others. Brown is a consummate

teller of stories. He sees men and women direct with his own eyes, as Chaucer and Shakespeare saw them. He understands them all because he loves them all. All his characters are of the broadly human type, nothing exceptional, nothing morbid. They show the permanent emotions and passions of human nature; and all are put before us with a love which glorifies and sanctifies what is common and natural.

Brown finds his material for poetry largely in the everyday life of working folk. There are some people, as we know, who think the daily life, the common talk, the homely ways of working folk, below the dignity of literature. They think that all who work with their hands—sailors, farm-hands, weavers, shoemakers, and the like—are commonplace, inartistic, vulgar. They are mistaken. Art and poetry find their true and perennial inspiration in humble homes and simple life, not in that which is artificial and conventional. 'Good society' has been sarcastically defined 'as that which affords no material for art or literature'. And the genius of the artist lies in his revealing to our dull eyes the loveliness in common scenes, and in common lives that are being lived all around us. Browning, in *Fra Lippo Lippi*, says most truly

> We're so made that we love
> First when we see them painted, things we have passed
> Perhaps a hundred times nor cared to see.

An artist paints an outline of moorland; a misty London street, with gas-lights reflected in its wet pavements; two working folk with bowed head, and the distant church tower, black against the evening sky; and he straightway opens our eyes to the beauty and pathos of such scenes. So does T. E. B. open our eyes to what few can see without such help, the human lovableness, or let us say more truly the presence of the Divine, in men and women of simple life, of rough exterior, and slow and rugged speech. It is a revelation for which we may thank God. All who know the *Fo'c's'le Yarns* will know what I mean. Which of us is not the better for knowing Tom Baynes, and the Pazon, and the Docthor, and Little Katty, and Mrs Cain and Tommy Gelling? Thank God for such pictures I say. They help us to recognise and honour such folk where we might never have suspected them. There are dear old Tom Baynes's on our quays; there are sweet Betsy Lees, and adorable Mrs Cains, in many a cottage.

Perfectly to reproduce such life and character involves the use of dialect; dialect is to the literary presentation of the life and genius of a people what suitable costume is on the stage of a theatre. Tom Baynes in Tennysonian English would be like Julius Caesar in a dress coat. Dialect for some literary purposes is indispensable. But it has too commonly come to be looked down upon as the mark of an illiterate person. Sir Walter Scott and Burns have secured literary rank for the Scotch dialect. But this rank has scarcely been won for any other. Edwin Waugh in Lancashire, Lowell in the United States, but more than all others Brown in the Isle of Man, have helped to break down this prejudice. Dialect is an unsurpassable instrument for expressing natural feeling. It is racy, terse, picturesque. It can say in a phrase what would take a sentence to express in literary language, and in that form would have lost its edge. The literary value of dialect is no new discovery. It is as old as Longinus. It was said by Montaigne that he would rather have his son learn the talk of the tavern than that of a school of elocution. 'In the tavern', he said, 'my son will learn directness, simplicity, and in these is the life of expression whether in speech or essay or poetry.' So when Lowell wanted to stir the soul of the United States of America in the war against slavery he wrote his *Biglow Papers* in the New England dialect, and he gave the reason why:

> I love the unhigh-schooled way
> Ol' farmers hed when I wuz younger;
> Their talk wuz meatier, an' 'ould stay,
> While book froth seems to whet your hunger:

Fer putting in a downright lick
'Twixt Humbug's eyes, there's few can metch it,
An' then it helves my thoughts ez slick
Ez stret-grained hickory does a hetchet.

So in Brown's stories the language fits the people; it is the language of common life, redolent of the fo'c's'le and the farm, with all the Keltic raciness of idiom. It is inconceivable that the stories should be told otherwise. Each phrase is inevitable. Let anyone try to turn a few lines of one of Brown's Yarns into literary English. He might as well try it with Burns' 'For Auld Lang Syne, my dears, for auld lang syne'. The spirit will have evaporated. The thought is wedded to the language, and it ought not to be forgotten that dialects are indispensable to students of early English, and they are made accessible only by such scholars as T. E. Brown. It is, moreover, certain that Anglo-Manx dialect is dying out. The far greater facilities for communication between England and the Island, and between the towns and countryside, and the all-unifying influence of elementary schools are killing dialect.

Revisiting the Island after twenty-four years I noticed in the country children I have talked to, indeed in all but the oldest generation, that a difference of intonation and speech has come over the Island. In a few generations, as Trafford Clegg says of his beloved Lancashire dialect, 'only a few scraps and relics of it will remain, like fossils on a beach'.

Brown has done a service to future students of the English language by seizing and preserving imperishably the Anglo-Manx dialect before it is for ever irrecoverably lost.

But all this is incidental. He wrote without any such far-off purpose. He wrote for Manxmen primarily.

Na'th'less for mine own people do I sing
And use the old familiar speech;
Happy if I shall reach
Their inmost consciousness.

6-2

With reference to Brown's lyrical and reflective poems, I personally hold these to be the greatest monument of his genius. They are finished, both in form and substance, and are happily free from that 'neo-obscurantism', to use Brown's own phrase, 'which seems to be settling down so fatally on modern literature'. They will assuredly live and be treasured, perhaps by the few, not only for their beauty, but as a contribution to the religious insight and thought of the world. In an age of religious questioning and re-construction, Brown was one of the few who could fearlessly probe to the bottom all questions, because he felt his feet planted on a rock. It was not the rock of authority in any form; but the rock of personal experience, of what can only be described as intimate and direct communing with God in Nature and his own soul. To convey some conception of this communing, to interpret to others their own vague and speechless moods and longings as the germ of such communing, is the highest function of poetry. In this sense Brown was not only a poet and a seer, but also a prophet and teacher—a teacher of theology; not from its formal and logical side, which never attracted him, but from the poetical and spiritual side, starting from no axioms but interrogating his own consciousness. No man was ever more full of faith in God, and in God's universal presence. The thinnest of veils, impenetrable however and impassable, seemed to separate him from that Presence.

Readers of his poems will recall his *Land-ho! Land*, and many others. He always had the reposeful assurance that

> A Power is working still on our behalf,
> A primal Power that in the world abides.

The intense faith that inspired his lyrics can only be understood by those who know and love them. I will not attempt to quote or expound them. His faith, though in some moods pantheistic, as it is called, is never otherwise than Christian. You will feel this intensely Christian faith in the *Hymn for Ascensiontide*, which is, unfortunately, omitted from his Collected Works. It can be seen in the Clifton College Hymn Book.[1] No one more truly loved our Church's time-honoured prayers—'well known at the gates of heaven', as old Fuller says—or more highly valued the continuity of soul-life, which those prayers imply and sustain. But I think he was independent of all such accessories to religion; he knew that there were moods in all men, moods not of one sort only, when these and all religious forms are inadequate and illusory; either, on the one hand,

> When the irregular grips
> Of zeal constrain the cleric breast or laic,
> Into a thousand fiery shreds it rips
> Our old Mozaic—

or when, on the other hand, God's inconceivability, as in the *Respondet Δημιουργός*, or the infinite and sorrowful mystery of human life pressed on his soul. To quote one passage only:

> One thing appears to me—
> The work is not complete;
> One world I know and see;
> It is not at His feet.
> Not, not? is this the sum?
> Not, not? the heavens are dumb.
> I bear His stigmata,
> Or not? ah, who shall say?
> Only it is most meet that I be sad,
> Sad, Sad!

Yes, he had many moods. But the permanent impression he left on his friends, with his far-reaching influence at Clifton College, was one of moral strength, intellectual vigour, and unshakable faith in the Divine, invisible guiding Hand. He flooded all life with light and truth and generous sympathies. He was one in whose presence meanness and shams and shallow sneering at faith were impossible. Such is the picture his strong individuality left on all who knew him.

[1] And in this volume on p. 205.

His day will come, if indeed it has not already come; and I trust that the centenary of his birth may contribute to establish him in the heart of the Manx people, in Ellan Vannin and scattered throughout the world, and to all who love the beautiful and the true. Happy are those who have learned to love and enjoy Brown's poems; and happiest of all are those who also loved and enjoyed the man himself.　　We shall not look upon his like again.

J. M. W.

STEEP
PETERSFIELD
October 23rd, 1928

II*

IMPRESSIONS OF T. E. BROWN

by

SIDNEY T. IRWIN

I may be allowed perhaps to say something from my own experience of the rarest personality that it has been my fortune to be acquainted with. In some respects I was disqualified for the fullest intimacy. For one thing I was, in his own phrase, *in partibus* im*musicorum*, and that was the gentlest of his phrases about this deficiency. Then his poems in dialect, though I enjoyed them, never appealed to me as his last volume did, and this should have been, to a less generous man, another disqualification.

Of the sea again, the object of his passionate devotion, I knew nothing as I ought to know. This *egotism*[1] is, I hope, pardonable, for it is necessary if I am to explain how his many-sided nature could so support an unequal friendship that the inequality was hardly felt.

I had been some two years at Clifton before I got to know Brown: but after our intimacy began I found fresh occasion for wonder every year at some new revelation of character and capacity. The first thing that not unnaturally invited friendship was his extraordinary gift of sympathy. The small things which interested his friends—the small pleasures and the small pains—were never below his reach. The merest fragment of 'coterie speech' was worth explaining to him.

* This and the following section are taken, by kind permission of Messrs Constable and Co., from the Introduction to *Letters of Thomas Edward Brown*, edited by Sidney T. Irwin, 1900.

[1] Mr Oakeley [whose reminiscences follow, App. III] apologising for himself may apologise for others also: 'One divines of one so rich and bounteous that to each of his friends he gave a different fortune.... Thus I seek to prepare the way for the otherwise crude remark, "None knew him as I did"' (Letter on hearing of Brown's death).

You were so certain of his gauging its significance to you. *Humani nihil a me alienum puto* was the motto of his talk as of his letters; but *humani* is not enough to say, for the personal interest went far beyond that, and this is one reason why so many of the letters to friends can only be represented by extracts. He gave himself without stint, his time, his thought, his powers; but the self was the greatest gift of all. That best self—its humour, its brilliance, its infinite variety—was all poured out for the single friend. Indeed the single friend was more likely to get that best than a large company, for he said of himself, as Cowper did, that he had a large stock of silence always at command, and this silence was more commonly seen in large companies.

He was just the man for unequal friendships. Nothing that he ever said or did would hint to one that he thought of himself as a shade better than his fellows. Only when one had time to reflect on an evening with him or a walk with him in which he had flashed into phrase after phrase or fancy after fancy, did it suddenly strike one that these novelties were all individual, that they were all different expressions of one and the same personality, and that neither your optimism nor your experience had prepared you for meeting such a man in ordinary life—'a man that would be incredible had one not known him', as FitzGerald said of Spedding. One can be grateful now, one could not then, for the illusion of equality was never disturbed.

One is conscious now of much self-reproach, thinking of all the chances of enlargement, and the scant use made of them: then one only thought of enjoyment. They were times of refreshing to look back to all one's life:

> Or other worlds they seemed, or happy isles.

But apart from the courtesy and generosity, the affection and consideration, which drew from all who called him friend the tribute of admiring love, there was that which made the merest acquaintance stand at gaze; something 'elemental, absolute, infallible'—to use three of his favourite adjectives about great men and great things. When he thus 'let himself go', he would characterise things and persons with truthfulness so vivid or paradox so grotesque that delight was almost smothered in gasping astonishment. His humour was then at the top of its bent, and his mimicry simply indescribable. I have watched him while he altered his face almost, and his voice wholly beyond recognition, when he was personating someone in a story he was telling. Mimicry is indeed possible to very common natures; but theirs is 'the mirth without images' of which Rasselas speaks. Brown's mimicry was often caricature, but it was the caricature of an overflowing imagination, not the caricature of a photograph. He could be Rabelaisian too at times, though always with a reservation very characteristic of him. 'There are', he said, 'nice Rabelaisians, and there are nasty Rabelaisians; but the latter are *not* Rabelaisians.'

Here, as elsewhere, nothing human, no one phase of human nature's many moods, was alien to him.

There was something too which seemed to separate him from other men in the kind and degree of his sympathy with external nature. He was himself conscious of this to some extent, and has expressed it in his letters (I think he is speaking of a late spring day in his beloved marsh country, the Curragh). 'These are the times', he said, 'when my highest power comes to me.'

Nor shall I ever forget his ecstasy over Fair Head in the County Antrim when we visited it together in 1895. It was worth going many miles to see.

This feeling of intimacy with external nature was one he cherished very carefully. 'I like', he said, 'to stay in a country till I know it in and out. That is far more to me than seeing many places.'

But whatever this intimacy was, it was not like his other gifts. One felt oneself outside; one looked on, one could not share. As one friend said, 'He seemed in possession of some great secret of nature which he was not free to impart to us'.

Another thing that was quite unlike anything I have known in others was the universal quality of his literary sympathy, and its intensity. This did more than anything else to establish our friendship; for though vast tracts of literature where he could 'rest and expatiate' were unknown to me, my own meagre domain seemed larger and richer when he expounded our common affection for it. 'Expounded' is a very poor word—though it is something to have the best reasons given for the faith that is in you, even when you feel your instinct beyond and above criticism.

But really it was nothing that could be called exposition. It was the spontaneous outflow of feeling deeper than one's own because the whole nature was deeper:

> And while we others sip the obvious sweet,
> . . .Lo! this man hath made haste
> And pressed the sting that holds the central seat.

It was no creed to be recited, it was an atmosphere in which he lived and breathed, that highest of all literary atmospheres, where the ingredients are all the humanities—love, respect, admiration, all clinging to the most sacred tradition of civilised man. 'Suffer no chasm', he once said to the School in a sermon, 'to interrupt this glorious tradition. . . . Continuous life. . . that is what we want—to feel the pulses of hearts that are now dust.'

'I could cry', he once said to me, 'over those old classical hymns of Addison.' The classical conventions moved him even while they amused him. He smiled, but the water stood in his eyes.

I do not think I have ever known a pleasure greater than finding some great or good thing in literature that he did not happen to know. Such occasions were few, as might be expected, but the pleasure was hardly less when one revived an old affection for him—a forgotten favourite.

And his analysis of beauties—when he would stoop to analysis, for he did not love 'to reason about beauties rather than to taste them'—never failed to satisfy.

I once drew his attention to the beautiful phrase of Steele, in the *Tatler*, about Favonius, the good clergyman, leaving the house of mourning 'with such a glow of grief and of humanity upon his countenance'. 'Ah, yes!' he said, 'and it's the *hendiadys* that does it!' and one feels at once how poor *humane grief* would sound beside it!

But independently of literature all associations moved him, and not his own merely. That is why 'coterie speech' had such a value for him. And he loved to have the fact or the legend out of which it sprang recovered for him with all its details. There was something specially delightful in the ease with which he could transplant, from another's experience, a story or a saying, and regrow it in his own more fertilising soil. It is no wonder that he had friends, for such common possessions rivet an intimacy as nothing else can.

His own associations were, it need hardly be said, all deep-rooted. His favourite Virgilian saw was *Antiquam exquirite matrem*, and he seemed to think the chief value of his poems was 'the cairn of memories' he had built in them. Even quite local and temporary associations were sacred to him. He saw his past steadily, and saw it whole, and the historical past he saw in the same way. 'In reading', he once said, 'let heart reach to heart across all obstacles of time, and manners, and ideas.'

I cannot but think that this was a great part of the meaning he assigned to his favourite text: 'Keep thy heart with all diligence'. He knew that the bent of intellect might shift with reading or experience; temper might be liable to moods, and disappoint either himself or others; but this other thing—the τὸ κυριώτατον, the heart, the proper self—

> That imperial murex grain
> No carrack ever bore to Thames or Tiber—

this must be cherished for what it was, must be still in a sense what it was—a self that vicissitude could not invade.

It was naturally not a thing he spoke of, but there were hints of it, to those who knew him, even in his talk; and in some of the letters, and in many of the poems in his last volume, it needs little interpretation to discover it. From the heart in this sense it is an easy transition to the 'kind of enthusiasm' with which uncommon men 'mingle their ideas'. In family affection, in friendship, in patriotism local or national, the sentiment is the same. It is not only *quorum pars magna fui*; it is also, 'what these things have made of me nothing can unmake'.

Under the impelling force of these associations he unshrinkingly confessed himself emotional, even using the half-humorous phrase, 'I am a born sobber'.

His fine curiosity was insatiable, but this was something related in no way to advances in knowledge or new refinements in feeling. It was something permanent and central to himself and yet universal in its range.

There is a beautiful passage in George Eliot's *Middlemarch*, where[1] Dorothea, asked what she is thinking of, says, 'All the troubles of all the people in the world'. Now it might be thought that, with Brown's high spirits and recklessly gay humour, this is a singularly inapposite quotation. But really it is very relevant. I have never known a man with so wide an intellectual range, or of such infinite brightness, who could be so deeply saddened by his own sympathies —sympathies reaching far back into his own far past, or extended to present trouble, ever so remote from himself.

This, I think, is the heart which he tried to keep with all diligence —the depth which he suffered no excursions of fancy to explore, no exuberance of spirits to disturb.

Of his life in this region—of the life of his lonelier self—not many, if any, of his friends were permitted to see much, yet it interfered in no way with his readiness to render all kinds of services. Those

---

[1] Quoted from memory. The *ipsissima verba* run thus: 'Dodo, how bright your eyes are!...I wonder what (has happened)'....'Oh, all the troubles of all people on the face of the earth.'

services rendered in abundant measure were much: but to possess
a sense of security, a recognised claim to divide pleasures and pains
without misgiving, was a thing beyond all price in friendship. That
this should be possible to one who had so full a life of his own
unshared, and not to be shared, by others, means a very rare un-
selfishness. Nor did he suffer such claims to be weakened by absence.
For the five years that remained to him after he returned to his Island
his letters never failed. He was never oppressed by the labour of
keeping friendships in repair, but rather exhilarated; at any rate he
left his friends exhilarated and something more. Those who received
his letters found in them such a store of help, such a heightening of
the interest of life, that to others—to those who had not enjoyed his
personal talk—it might have seemed that little could have been added
by actual intercourse.

Brown was a keen critic of all his friends, and did not deny himself
amusement at the weaknesses and limitations of those he cared for
most. But there was one thing about him not often found in men
who indulge in the mood of Democritus. I mean the willingness to
take trouble for those whose failings amused him, even when he
thought there was some connection between their unwisdom and
their need. I don't think he could for the life of him help giving
free play to his humour, but it never weakened his friendship. He
was even so anxious in their behalf as to transform himself on occasion
into what he once called 'Machiavelli Brown', and draw on his
experience to play the diplomatist in their interest. His courtesy
would never suffer him to be the candid friend. In these matters he
contended for what he called 'the finest Keltic make-believe', and
was indignant at its being confounded with 'humbug'. ('Oh, those
English!' he would say.) To him this 'finest make-believe' was a
part of the code of good manners, and if he criticised his friends to
others, they knew better than those others how little it impaired his
power to love and his eagerness to serve.

To manners he always attached a value which is less common in these days. 'If I lose my manners', he said once over some trivial forgetfulness, 'what is to become of me?'

But the thing that will stay longest with his friends was the amount and variety of positive pleasure that he gave them. Five minutes in his company was a more exhilarating tonic than any that could be devised. Tonic is the right word, for more than one reason, when his talk was of literature: for his sanity was as steadying to the judgment as his enthusiasm was lifting to the spirit. If there was a side of literature that appealed less to him than to others, I can find no word less inclusive than catholic to do justice to his range of sympathy. And his catholicity of taste was especially remarkable in one whose strength of imagination might be supposed to have made him somewhat impatient of the ancient ways and the less ambitious ages when writers were content 'to dwell quiet and secure'. While he welcomed power in every new direction, his faith in the old teachers, the *pauci quos aequus amavit Iuppiter*, never swerved.

In the Sermon from which I have already quoted he preached his own practice. 'Those', he said, 'who have been and are great amongst us are those who have dwelt most reverently, or at least most habitually, under the shadow of the sky-pointing pyramids of the past.'

But I must not go on. I have already, perhaps, said too much, though in another sense too much could not be said.

> 'Tis true; but all too weakly said;
> 'Twas more significant, he's dead.

There is a simple sentence in another letter-writer, not often so simple, who very occasionally recalls Brown, though with a difference; and this sentence—it is Charles Lamb's—tells Brown's friends better than any words of their own what their individual loss is, and why they can never see his place filled for them.

'One sees a picture, reads an anecdote, starts a casual fancy, and thinks to tell of it to this person in preference to every other. The person is gone whom it would peculiarly have suited—it won't do for another.'

III

REMINISCENCES OF T. E. BROWN

by

E. M. OAKELEY

Looking back on my friendship with Mr Brown, which began a very few days after I became a Clifton master in 1867, and knew no break till the great break in October, 1897, I realise only too keenly, now that he is gone, 'the difference to me'. Many, of course, are feeling the same; yet not quite the same, for it may easily be guessed that a nature so rich and so bounteous as his showed a different side to each friend, so that many can without arrogance say, 'No one knew him as I did'. Of late I had seen him but seldom, but I continued to hear from him pretty often till very near his end; and for the rest, as he once wrote to me, 'there are people with whom to coexist is life: no need to see them or talk to them. All that is needed is just to think—say in your bath at 7 a.m.—"Hugh also is"'.

Mr Brown's love of music was a side of him often turned to the present writer, and music was a chief corner-stone of our friendship. In early Clifton days I induced him to go up with me to hear Clara Schumann play; a memorable experience in many ways, not least from our accidentally sitting next to Madame Jenny Lind-Goldschmidt, to whom, as he reminded me as lately as October, 1897, I took the opportunity to introduce him. At about the same date, by the way, we went, with Dr Percival, to see the Clifton match at Lord's, the chief hero of which was just then the pride of Brown's House at Clifton, as afterwards of his College and University.[1] T. E. B. was

---

[1] Cecil William Boyle, the 'dear hero' of a poem contributed to *The Spectator* by his school-fellow, T. [now Sir] Herbert Warren, then President of Magdalen. He fell at Boshof, April 5, 1900,

'Captaining men as once he captained boys'.

in great force, and lit up the dingy dining-room of our hotel—quite innocent then of to-day's Asiatic splendours—with many a flash of that 'lightning of the brain, lambent but innocuous', that one associates with his conversation.

It must have been in that same summer that I used to sit with him in the Fifth Form room of his house, in the holidays an uncommonly secluded *sanctum*, in order to discuss words and tunes for the School Hymn Book, on which a committee of masters and boys had been for some time at work. It was then and there that Wesley's fine hymn, with the recurring line 'Give me thy only love', was re-edited to make it fit Bach's soaring music, which seems to yearn to bear on its wings some such refrain as Wesley's. To the same *symposia* the hymn book owes Mr Brown's noble Ascensiontide hymn. It was agreed that the *tune* of '*Es ist das Heil*' must be secured for the book; but the ponderous unwieldiness of the German original, which refused on almost any terms to be carried over or coaxed into English, suggested the fortunate alternative—that 'someone' should write a new hymn, suitable to the peculiar sentiment, and especially to the pathetic closing cadence, of the music. No other hymn-tune was so dear to him, except perhaps the well-known *Passion Chorale*, of which—in a blue-pencilled note one Monday morning during first lesson—he sent me the following 'appreciation':

Ὠκλείῳ Βροῦνος. . . .

(Yesterday, when you were playing the miraculous 'Haupt'[1].)

> Chance-child of some lone sorrow on the hills,
> Bach finds a babe; instant the great heart fills
> With love of that fair innocence,
> Conveys it thence,
> Clothes it with all divinest harmonies,
> Gives it sure foot to tread the dim degrees

---

[1] The version played was No. 27, vol. v, of Bach's organ works. This is mentioned out of kindness prepense, that Bach-lovers may turn to it again. They will have their reward!

Preparation

Hast thou a cunning instrument of play,
'Tis well; but see thou keep it bright,
And tuned to primal chords, so that it may
    Be ready day and night:
For when He comes thou know'st not, who shall say—
"These virginals are apt," and try a note,
    And sit, and make sweet solace of delight,
Nor ever shall stand to list on the way,
    And all the room with heavenly music float.
                    Clifton Jun 9/75

Planting.

Who would be planted chooseth not the soil
    On here or there,
        On loam or peat
            Wherein he best may grow,
And bring forth guerdon of the planter's toil—
    The lily is most fair,
        But says it—"I will only blow
Upon a southern land;" the cedar makes no coil
        What rock shall owe
        The springs that wash his feet;
The crocus cannot arbitrate the foil
        That for its purple radiance is most meet—
        Lord, even so
I ask one prayer,
        The which if it be granted,
It skills not where
        Thou plantest me, only I would be planted.
                    Clifton Jun 4/75

Of Pilate's stair. Hush! Hush! Its last sweet breath
Wails far along the passages of death.

I quote this as a specimen of the writer's method of musical criticism; a method equally remote from the usual style of describers of music, the 'piling of honey on sugar and sugar on honey' (as Lamb writes in a slightly different connection), as from the heresy of the *Leit-Motif* fanatics who used to pester Mendelssohn to tell them 'the meaning' of his *Songs without Words*. So far was Brown from desiring to trace 'meanings' in instrumental music, that even in the *vocal* works of the great composers he held that the so-called setting was distinctly 'the predominant partner', and that, except as a crib for the unlearned, the words would often be better away. Thus, for instance, he writes of his own beautiful translation of those lines of Eichendorff which Schumann has immortalised by linking them to his *Frühlingsnacht*:

Here is the *Frühlingsnacht*—might be better, though I think it is not exactly bad....

Wandervögel is a lovely word. I suppose he does not mean birds *in* his garden, but birds passing over it, invisible, though audible to him. 'Birds of passage' is not altogether prosaic—incline thine ear, perpend, what thinkest? In the second verse I have imported a little wild-fire. The tune seems to comport it; but 'reappears' is an old rhyme-*famulus*, and it does not either comport or support the *ritardando* as well as *Mondes Glanz herein*. In fact I feel the German even to be rather lacking...and taking it altogether, don't you regard this song of Schumann's as transcending words—*Über Worte? Procul, O Procul!* The poets are not in it. I warn them off the ground. When Schumann is in this mood, they had better retire. The mysteries are too sacred, the *pudicitia* of the absolute ought not to be violated. It is divine—divine! Look at those wretched words as they sidle up in their smugness to the heavenly creature! What earthly right have they there? She does not want them. 'A parcel

of the purest sky',—that is the *Frühlingsnacht*. And this —— libretto
to think of holding his vulgar umbrella over her—faugh![1]

The translation follows:

A NIGHT OF SPRING

O'er the garden, northward yearning,
　　Birds of passage on the wing
Give the note of Spring's returning,
　　And the odours of the Spring.

Shall I shout for very gladness,
　　Shall I drown my eyes in tears,
Is it mirth, or is it madness,
　　When the spring-tide reappears?

Moon and stars proclaim her willing,
　　Whisp'ring groves their vows combine,
And the nightingales are thrilling—
　　'She is thine, ah, she is thine!'

Here is his translation of *Meine Rose*, another of Schumann's
loveliest songs:

MY ROSE

When Summer's sun is glowing,
And roses still are blowing,
If but I note one drooping,
Its lovely head down stooping,
I bring with timely shower
Refreshment to my flower.
Blest Rose, that art the dearest!
Heart's Rose, the sweetest, nearest,
O'erwhelm'd with care and sadness,
Ah me! the joy, the gladness
If, at thy feet outpouring,
My soul I lay adoring!

[1] To somewhat the same effect Philipp Spitta writes: 'In Schumann's songs
the function of the pianoforte is to reveal some deep and secret meaning which
is beyond the power of words to express'.

Life's self I would surrender
To see thee rise in splendour.[1]

Brown's method of musical criticism, in which (naturally!) the seemingly 'far-fetched' fancies of the poet convey an impression far more adequate than the usual attempt to describe the indescribable by mere inventory or mere superlatives, may be further illustrated by the following description of a Crystal Palace concert:

...I have said nothing about the choral *annexe* to the ninth symphony. No circumstances could be more unfavourable to a choir; when your ears have been stung for upwards of an hour by the most delicious string poison, 'the human voice divine' is simply grotesque. There is one passage where the tenors lead off. Well, it sounded almost like a poor melancholy laugh, as of idiots. And indeed they had not even their note quite true. Then you remember a chorus takes off suddenly, and leaves a quartet exposed in mid-field. This is a most exquisite machine, to my mind. It is as if a thunderstorm suddenly cleared away, and four stars shone out in a sweet quaternion of solitude. It ought to be that. A calm soft kiss on the forehead of retreating turbulence. But what did these people do? It was Winkle torn from Weller. They seemed so frightened: quite ghastly. Nothing to sit down on! And in such *impari materia*! Another stuff; not four threads spun finely, deftly forth from the big choral web, and streaming on a summer sigh of balm—but dingy floccy alien tatters tossed up obscenely from a dust-heap. Yet Alversleben seemed not inadequate; the others, so help me sweet Cecilia, did not know 'wherefore they were come together'!

And of another performance of the same symphony:

The absolutely celestial coda was now and then as unerring as I could desire; but once, if I mistake not, nearly fell to pieces. It was a fearful moment; as if your dearest and loveliest on earth were suddenly to totter on the verge of madness, and say wicked and impure words....Ophelia...I felt quite giddy. But it was soon over, and the darling shone out bright and calm and peerless as ever.

---

[1] 'The original seems to express despair of this result. I have not made it so strong. Any man, reducing himself to a watering-pot, has a right to expect success, or something of the kind'.—T. E. B.

What heavenly peace! What healing of all wounds! Binding of all broken hearts! Everlasting *remedium amoris*! I certainly found myself praying, and that fervently. With such a Christ to clasp to her withered breast, what need the poor old world care for Strauss and all his angels?

At the rehearsal of this concert:

It was even more interesting than the concert. Manns unfettered by the proprieties, mad, springing to his feet, hurling himself at the band like a tiger, like a thunderbolt, like a conical bullet, like a little black devil! A splendid and never-to-be-forgotten sight. I saw his dodges, and more or less comprehended them.

At a Crystal Palace organ recital:

There was Mr X. pounding away at some screaming indecency. I waited for his second piece, though much dejected, but as it was only some sugary or rather rum-and-sugary Operatic *rifacimento*, I came away, and left him up to his ears in Organ treacle....

(He returned, however; for—)

Smart's Andante in D is a pretty thing enough, not so much crisp as mincing. In our poor friend's hands it assumed an air of the fatuously dissolute.

On British musical taste, *circa* 1870, he writes:

We have been getting fonder of music, and of good music. In some fashion—rather haphazard, perhaps—we have been learning to know good music when we hear it. No doubt the middle-class drawing-room, that last fortress of error, is much where it was. Time-honoured shrine of die-away, sigh-away adolescence, it still resounds to the strains of the Valérie Whites and the Molloys. But the Teutonic invasion has told; Mendelssohn has almost obtained the Britannic *civitas*, and even Schumann stands—uncertain, it is true—upon the threshold. And if we pass from the drawing-room to the concert hall, the state of affairs is positively encouraging. Here are great organs magnificently played; here is Bach; here is a band; here are Beethoven, Berlioz, Wagner, all the gods....

In 1894 Brown made a much-looked-forward-to pilgrimage to Bayreuth; of which he writes (before starting):

I am to hear *Lohengrin*, *Tannhäuser*, and *Parsifal* (the last, twice). This will be a good βάπτειν in the Wagnerian Siloam.

(From Bayreuth:)

I am waiting here for a *noch einmal* of *Parsifal*. But you may depend on it that the *cultus* is a little unsound. Talk is big, and make-believe bigger; but they don't do the business so superlatively well by any means. . . .

(After the *noch einmal*:)

Won't do! *Parsifal* is an impossibility, and I am hugely disappointed. . . . Set to your seal that the musical drama is a tremendous but hopeless aspiration. Fall back upon Beethoven and the symphonic form, and take courage. I don't wonder at men thinking that this is a path that no one can tread after Beethoven. But this is wrong. The world is open: we can gather the flowers of Heaven. Not, however, in this field of combination and complication will they ever be gathered. . . . Wagner's *Wahn*—exactly so, a noble *Wahn*, but brings me no *Friede* as Wagner says it did to him—will bring *Friede* to no child of man who is born with wings, however imperfectly developed.

(After returning:)

Have you heard that there are to be orchestral Wagner concerts in London next November, the first to be conducted by Siegfried Wagner? That is just what I should like. The man Curtius is trying to arrange with Madame Wagner for the production of substantial portions of *Parsifal*. *Orchestral*, remember! That's the point. As to their lewdness and superfluity of scenic naughtiness, may I never again come within a hundred miles of them!

From Music to Mimicry, even if the two gifts be not wholly unrelated, may perhaps seem an abrupt transition. But however that may be, one cannot long think of Brown without recalling his mimicry. (His own abrupt transitions by the way—say from Bach to Balzac—used to be sufficiently amusing!) Was there one of his acquaintances whom he could not reproduce to the very life? Nay, his portraiture was in a sense *more* vivid than life, because it gave the type and idea of the man, and not merely the man himself, who might well (if modest) feel himself but a poor pale counterfeit of Brown's revised version of him, and say on being told of it (as I once heard him say), 'Well, I did not say quite that, but *I would have said so if I had thought of it*'. Quite so; in a word, of most people Brown's rendering was better far than their own! What portraits one's memory retains of Clifton masters, boys, servants—not so much printed there from life, as due to some of those almost proverbial 'five minutes with Brown in the masters' room'!

And no account of his mimicry would be complete, without adding that, 'irrespective of sex or age', he could to a wonderful degree even *look* like his subject of the moment.

How utterly without malice it all was, may be divined from the following:

...Truest and dearest of friends! My foster-father! Source of perennial joy, of laughter inextinguishable. I have mimicked him all my life, and shall I forbear now? Nay, verily, and by God's help so I won't. I did love that old man; a delicious old man: Silenus trimmed with Socrates, and turned up with ...well...I don't mind, say Newman.

Often in reading his letters over, one longs to *hear* that delightful mimicry again.

Mr W. was present, an invaluable grotesque. He preached the sermon—I will venture to say the most ludicrous performance of modern times. Anything like the hodge-podge of imbecility, except its author, I have never seen. This phenomenon has awaked my long-dormant faculty of mimicry; I can't refrain. Such a heaven-sent subject is not to be lighted upon every day.

And sometimes one *does* all but hear it:

Their chief pastor, good man, is—well, he *is*, and that is about all that can be said. They are good worthy people; probably never open a book, a piano, or—yes, he has opened a bazaar—two bazaars, I think. Oh yes! we can do that—yes! 'yess, indeet, however'.

IV

T. E. B.

by

SIR HERBERT WARREN, K.C.V.O.

SOMETIME PRESIDENT OF MAGDALEN
COLLEGE, OXFORD

When I passed to Clifton in January, 1868, at the age of fifteen, from a private school (a very good one of its kind but of rather an amateur character), I was struck by the difference of the boys but still more by the difference of the masters. They seemed so much more professional, authoritative, confident in their position and themselves. They were the officers of an army, not the assistants in a private business. At first I only came across and began to know two or three. There was of course 'Jupiter Olympius', the Headmaster, Dr Percival, awful, aloof, supreme. I had been viewed and orally examined by him in the Sixth Form Room where he sat presiding over those heroes, the Sixth Form; but except for one chance interview later I only saw and heard him at a distance all through my first year, till at the end of it I too entered the heroic circle. My first Form Master, J. M. Marshall, and my Mathematical Master, Charles Cay, and the very German Dr Debus, head of the Chemical Laboratory, I soon got to know and to make friends with; this too a novel experience. The rest were figures whom we saw moving about and heard of from other boys.

But there was one who stood out for us all, T. E. Brown. He was the largest planet and the nearest to the sun. He was 'Head of the Modern Side'. An occasion came when Dr Percival had to be absent. Brown read prayers in Big School and began to 'call over'. There was a certain cat's-away feeling among the Fourth and Third Forms. Suddenly Brown's voice rang out, 'Who's making that disturbance? —Some small fry on the Classical Side, I think'. The shot went home and we subsided, and I became interested in Brown. It was his voice that had arrested me, rich, melodious, thunderous when he liked, but distinctly appealing, the musical utterance of an organ of many notes.

And he himself was impressive and imposing; a fine head, large and strong but set on strong shoulders and frame, the capital of a worthy pillar. He fascinated me. At the concerts I heard him sing, both in solos and with others, and again enjoyed his musical voice and individual expression.

When I got into the Sixth I began to hear of him from companions who were in his Form Room or in his House, from Robert Don and Cecil Boyle. 'He was great at English and History.' 'He was a martinet ruling with a strong hand.' Then someone whispered that withal he was a practising poet. This excited my interest; but still I did not know him. One odd *rencontre* I remember. He was moving slowly towards his room at the inner end of the long cloisters. A master, short-sighted, at the other end, saw him and called out, 'Porter! Porter!' Brown half turned towards me and said in his deep voice, 'The foolish fellow, he doesn't know Porter from Brown Stout'.

Still he remained aloof, but perhaps all the more an interesting figure. Very rarely—about once a year—he would preach in the School Chapel. His sermons were something of an event. His language, like his voice, was rich and full of many notes and colours. 'A good School should be a social *eranos*', he said in one of these. I had just learnt the meaning of the word. It never occurred to me that it could be used in English. Again I was fascinated.

Later arrived days when I began to know well Dakyns and Oakeley, and through them I heard yet more of this still mysterious personage and poet. Then came my intimacy with J. A. Symonds, and I found that Brown was one of his literary coterie, interchanging poems and criticisms on life and letters. One of the earliest things Brown did at Clifton was to offer an annual prize for an English poem. In my last year the subject was 'Oxford' and I was lucky enough to gain the prize. I have recently presented my MS, which I kept and which bore some pencil marks of T. E. B. upon it, to the School Library. I may perhaps be pardoned for being specially pleased that on the cover he had written 'Tandem, T. E. B.'

But it was only after I had left the School that in the vacations when I was at home I ventured to '*abord*' him myself. I used to join him in walks around Clifton. There was one I specially remember because it began on Redland Green, where stands that trim, prim, little classical eighteenth-century church, which I had just begun to appreciate—with the churchyard where he was in the end to be buried—and went by byways and backways across fields to Durdham Down. He talked now no longer to me as a boy but as man to man, and I found him original, humorous, startling in his freedom of range and remark. I think it was about this time that I learned that he had for a time taken clerical duty in the squalid and immoral region of the Hotwells alluded to in one of his poems. This both increased and heightened my admiration.

After he had left Clifton he appeared, I don't exactly remember when or why, in Oxford; and came to see me and proposed that we should stroll to Addison's Walk. When we came to just where that walk begins, opposite the Holywell-Ford Mill, Brown stopped and looked at the mill for some time, and then told me that he had a special association with it dating from his undergraduate days. What it was he did not reveal. When, after his death, his poems were published and I came on the charming little piece headed *An Oxford Idyll* and subscribed 'Magdalen Walk', I understood at once. The shy, struggling, studious, poetic servitor of ChristChurch shortly to take his Double First had known and poeticised like others his 'Miller's Daughter'.

> When she was true, and twenty-two,
> And I was two-and-twenty

would make the date 1852–3.

The poem itself, however, would appear to have been written on May the 24th, 1875, and prefaced by a note 'All that I got at Oxford'!

His degree was a singularly brilliant one. He took a First Class in 'Greats' in the Summer Term of 1853 along with Frederic Harrison and F. W. Walker, later High Master of St Paul's, and in the autumn of the same year stood alone in the First Class in Law and History. One other recollection of his Oxford days came to me, I think from Dr Fowler of C.C.C. It was known how unusual he was, and Thorold Rogers brought in Cobden to hear his *viva voce* and witness what a young Oxford student could do.

I have always thought that the best description of him as he was when I knew him is that given by H. F. Brown (no relation) in his Introduction to the Golden Treasury *Selections* and the best single epithet applied to him that of Dr Percival, 'Volcanic'.

HERBERT WARREN

V

'BROWN'S HOUSE'

SOME MEMORIES

by

PROFESSOR F. S. BOAS

M.A. (OXON.); HON. LL.D. (ST ANDREWS)

The Brown Centenary Committee have invited me to contribute to the Centenary Volume in honour of T. E. Brown, whose House at Clifton I entered in September, 1877. It is a pleasure to me to take any part in such a publication. But I believe that it will be most to the purpose if I confine myself to personal memories, and make no attempt at an estimate of Brown's literary work. For that, I hope, we may look in this volume to its Editor. And I shall elsewhere, as it happens, have an opportunity of dealing with the wider aspects of Brown's career and achievement. Last year the Royal Society of Literature published a volume, edited by Mr H. Granville-Barker, containing lectures by a number of its Fellows on *The Eighteen-Seventies*. This year a similar volume will be edited by Mr Walter de la Mare on *The Eighteen-Eighties*, and as *Fo'c's'le Yarns*, *The Doctor* and *The Manx Witch* appeared during that decade, I propose in my own contribution to take T. E. Brown as the subject. I hope that I may be furthering the aims of the Brown Centenary Committee by thus attempting to bring home the significance of his poetic and educational work to some who have no links with it, either through Clifton or the Isle of Man.

But here I am writing, in the first place, for those who have such personal ties, and who will be interested in what I may call domestic memories. And fortunately I have not to trust entirely to my present-day recollections. All readers of *The Times Literary Supplement* may not remember that it had a predecessor called *Literature*.

In this journal on November the 17th, 1900, soon after the publication of Brown's *Collected Poems* and of his *Letters*, edited by his colleague S. T. Irwin, I had an article on 'Brown's House'. As it is now doubtless forgotten, and as my memory of my schooldays had a keener edge thirty years ago, I have drawn freely upon it. But I have added, omitted, and altered, and have carried on the tale briefly into the present century.

My first meeting with Brown was, as I have said above, in September, 1877. I was a shy newcomer to Clifton, fresh from an Irish school, and after all these years I have an ineffaceable memory of the impression of mingled strength and geniality which his presence at once inspired. As he was Head of the 'Modern Side' at Clifton, his House was composed mainly of boys on that 'Side'. Like most boys going to Oxford or Cambridge I was on the 'Classical Side', and I therefore never came under Brown as a Form Master, and cannot speak at first-hand of his powers as a teacher. But his commanding personality left its impress upon all the boys who were under his charge as House-master. It was, in the main, the energy and breezy vigour of his complex nature rather than his distinctively intellectual gifts that were reflected in 'Brown's House'. If there are any admirers of his verse who have formed fanciful pictures of a poetic master training up a band of youthful literary aspirants, they may be surprised to hear that, though our House had always its full share of scholastic honours, its dominant passion was to become Cock House at football, and especially to triumph over the School House, between which and 'Brown's' there was a traditional rivalry. The first occasion on which this distinction had been achieved was when Cecil Boyle, as Head of the House, led his team to victory. To us of a later generation he was a hero of almost legendary prowess, and the gallant death in April, 1900, in the South African War, of this 'young Achilles of the field', as he was called in a touching elegy by his friend and contemporary, Sir Herbert Warren, seemed a fitting climax to the achievements of his school career. Another Head of the House, Charles Cannan, afterwards to become the eminent Secretary to the Delegates of the Clarendon Press, did much to foster the keenly public-spirited tradition of 'Brown's'. When I was a new boy the Secretary of the School introduced me to him, and he gave me a characteristically blunt warning to behave myself, unless I wanted to be 'kicked out' of the House. I sometimes reminded him of this in later years, when we were talking over books in his office at the Clarendon Press. It was, at any rate, a satisfaction to Cannan when, during my own headship of the House and captaincy of the team, we repeated the triumph of Boyle's day on the football field. And it was almost the proudest moment of my life when Boyle himself, in honour of the event, came down to the annual House-supper and spoke to me, not from some lofty Olympian height, but simply as 'man to man'.

Brown's letters prove that he was not the type of schoolmaster who unduly magnifies games; but he took a genuine interest and pride in the athletic achievements of his boys. And though by his genius and his temperament he was an opponent of the orthodox and the conventional, he had no sympathy with the view that the routine of a great public school crushes out a boy's individuality. An address had one night been given to us emphasising this idea, which has of course had many later advocates since 'self-expression' became a current catch-word. But Brown at House-dinner on the following day expressed to me his strong dissent from such doctrine, and he even jocularly began to tag a few verses on the topic which ran something as follows:

> A boy, as a rule,
> At a public school
> Is a bit of a fool...

who does not join in the general life of work and play.

There were occasions, indeed, when his sense of the importance of corporate life and collective responsibility showed itself in a somewhat drastic way. It happened that a piece of furniture in the dining-room had been damaged. Brown announced that unless by a certain fixed time the boy who had committed the offence came forward, the whole House would be 'kept in' on the next half-holiday. The culprit did not confess, and all of us consequently, to the number of over forty, paid the penalty, Brown himself sharing our afternoon's detention. My own belief was, and is, that however the damage may have originated, it was not really due to any member of the House.

Such stringent exercises of authority were, however, very rare. As a rule, if anything were amiss, a few words from Brown, generally addressed to the House after evening prayers, were sufficient to set matters right. His picturesqueness and raciness of phrase were inexhaustible, and his talks to the House were nearly always illumined by some characteristic flash of humour or some apt literary allusion. On one occasion, soon after I entered the House, some boys had been detected in the nefarious practice of cooking in their studies. Brown kept us in roars of laughter while he depicted the scene, and wound up by comparing the culprits to the witches in *Macbeth* interrupted when engaged in their weird dance round their cauldron, with its grisly ingredients. His speeches, too, at the House-suppers were looked forward to by us with keen enjoyment. And at a time when he was in deep domestic sorrow he showed his lofty public spirit by insisting that the festivity should be held in the usual way.

Readers of Brown's poetry or of his letters know well his passion for the real, the elemental, at whatever cost. And in his daily talk, in his most off-hand judgments, the same strain was always present. Like most boys with an interest in literature I dabbled in rhyme at school, and Brown once asked to see some verses I had written— on a stock poetic theme which has escaped my memory. After a few words of comment on my production, he turned to me suddenly with the suggestion, 'Now try what you can do with an *unpoetic* subject—a chimney-sweep, for instance'. The chimney-sweep still remains, as far as I am concerned, one of the things 'unattempted yet in prose or rhyme', but my vision of the boundaries of song was forthwith enlarged. A different and later illustration of Brown's 'realistic' temper may interest the Editor of this Centenary Volume. Soon after 'Q' had begun his career as a novelist in 1887 with *Dead Man's Rock*, I had on a visit to Clifton a talk with Brown about the book. He spoke of it very appreciatively, but thought that the lover, when accepted, did not salute his lady with sufficient *empressement*.

But Brown's most characteristic 'adventure in criticism' that I remember was on the subject of hymns. An excellent institution at Clifton (I hope that it still survives) was a meeting of the boys on Sunday evenings in Big School. After the singing of a hymn, and the performance by E. M. Oakeley of some classical music on the organ, an address was given, generally by one of the masters, sometimes by a visitor. This, though known irreverently as 'a jaw', was highly popular. On one Sunday evening Brown discoursed on 'Hymns, considered from the literary and musical points of view'. The hymn that had been sung before his address happened to be Heber's 'From Greenland's icy mountains'. While allowing the words to pass muster with faint approval, he assailed unsparingly the tune to which they were set. He made caustic remarks about a number of other well-known hymns, denouncing them as sentimental or unreal. And the climax came when he parodied such lines as

> And for every blade of grass,
> Praise, O praise Him, as we pass!

by the trenchant couplet which has stuck in my memory for half a century:

> And for every pot of jam,
> Praise, O praise, the great I Am!

The boys, of course, enjoyed it all thoroughly, though it caused head-shaking by some of our elders. That Brown could appreciate fully hymns of what he considered true quality is shown by his enthusiasm for those of Charles Wesley and 'the old Evangelical school', and by the fact related by S. T. Irwin that Brown once sent him a hymn written by his father, the Vicar of Kirk Braddan, for which 'he had a feeling that could not be described as mere filial tenderness'.

But if Brown as a critic was thus known to the School at large, those of us who were members of his House had the rarer privilege of making his acquaintance at first-hand as a poet, though we did not at the time realise our good fortune. On Saturday evenings Brown from time to time gave the House a 'reading'. On one or two occasions we were surprised to hear him read poems of which none of us had heard, and which were in an unfamiliar dialect. Recited as they were in his rich and wonderfully flexible tones, and with keen dramatic power, they made a deep impression on us—even on those of us who had least care for poetry. We speculated as to their origin, and it was only in later days that we learnt that the reader of the poems was also their author. Brown, it is true, had already published *Betsy Lee* in 1873, but schoolboys could scarcely be expected to know of a 'local' poem which had not in the 'seventies made much noise in the world. It was not till 1881, the year in which I left Clifton, that it appeared in *Fo'c's'le Yarns*, with other tales in verse, of which Brown had given us a foretaste in his readings before they became the property of the public outside. And I imagine that he himself enjoyed watching the effect that he thus produced upon his 'young barbarians'. He could scarcely have put his work to a severer test; poetry, to impress the average schoolboy, must have the root of the matter in it. I would like to think that he remembered our youthful spontaneous homage to his genius when in later years he made his jest—yet not wholly a jest—that he was not included in a notice of the minor poets of his time, because, perhaps, he belonged to the major ones.

Except as an Old Cliftonian I have no personal ties with the West of England, and my visits to the School and the House since 1881 have been less frequent than I could have wished. But in 1884 I took down to Clifton my younger brother, H. J. Boas, when he was trying for an entrance scholarship, which he won. He entered

Brown's House in September, and eventually became both Head of the House and of the School. He passed direct from Clifton (under the old regulations) into the Indian Civil Service in 1889, and rose to be a Deputy Commissioner in the United Provinces before his premature death at Lucknow in May, 1910. To the last he had a feeling of devotion to the School and to 'Brown's'. His son, E. H. Boas, entered the House, which had now become 'Russell's', in September, 1917, and he too became Head of the School in 1922. Another nephew, E. G. Boas, who had preceded him as a member of 'Russell's' in January, 1913, was a subaltern in the Royal Irish Rifles, and was killed on the Somme, on July the 1st, 1916, a fatal date in the ears of Ulstermen.

Thus in person or through relations my connection with the 'House' spans nearly half a century. It has been known since by names honoured by every Cliftonian—Moore's, Asquith's, Russell's —but to me it will always be 'Brown's House', and I never felt this more than when during the College Jubilee of 1912 I lunched once again in the familiar hall, where I had heard Brown read his poems, and saw some of the old photographs upon the walls. It was in that hall, as Miss Ethel Brown remembers, that it fell to me, when I was Head of the House, to propose the health at the annual Supper of Mr and Mrs Brown. I compared Brown to Cleopatra, and then explained to my surprised hearers that it was because

> Age cannot wither him, nor Custom stale
> His infinite variety.

It was a schoolboy's adaptation of a famous passage. But I think that it has stood the test of time. Brown's variety was indeed astonishing. He was schoolmaster, cleric, poet, letter-writer, nature-lover, musician and wit. But one may be all these in a measure and not be great. In Thomas Edward Brown there was something elemental that fused together all his powers, and that will secure him, as those who passed under his influence hope and believe, an imperishable name.

F. S. BOAS

VI

BROWN

by

SIR HALL CAINE, K.B.E., C.H.

If I am to write ever so slight a sketch of Brown (and I am glad to be asked to do something), I must beg to be permitted to begin by speaking of him chiefly in relation to his interest in my own doings, or tryings-to-do, for, although our acquaintance covered more than eleven years, in hardly any other connection did I really and truly know him, so little did I contribute to our friendship and so much did he.

I had written two novels with their scenes in Cumberland, my mother's country, before I thought of carrying out a suggestion of Rossetti that I should try to become the novelist of Manxland. Then I went with my project to consult a famous Manxman of his day, the Rev. Hugh Stowell Brown.

Stowell Brown, who was my father's friend, disapproved of it altogether. 'Don't attempt it', he said. 'If you do, you will have a lasting disappointment. The readers of novels from circulating libraries don't care one straw about the Isle of Man. Nobody cares about it, and I would earnestly counsel you to abandon the idea.' In thus dismissing me with his wet blanket, Stowell Brown added, 'But if you MUST write about that God-forsaken little island you ought to go to my brother Tom'.

I did not go to his brother Tom, but with characteristic good-fellowship his brother Tom came to me, and thus began one of the tenderest and truest friendships of my life, my friendship with the racy, the brilliant, the entirely charming and delightful author of *Fo'c's'le Yarns*: the most loyal, the most generous, the most unselfish of men. If I quote from the letters he wrote to me at the beginning of our acquaintance more than one passage which modesty might call upon me to suppress, I shall do so with one object only—to reveal to the reader the large generosity, the measureless charity, the splendid, if too lavish, appreciativeness which made T. E. Brown, for all who knew him, the most fascinating of friends.

'It may be late', he wrote, 'but even so I must write to tell you with what pleasure I have read your Cumberland story. I think it is wholly delightful. The style too is admirable; in fact, it *is* a style, and a very fine one. We are now looking out, somewhat nervously, for a successor to George Eliot, and we should, many of us, be well content to see a successor to Mrs Gaskell. I feel that you belong to this rank of novelists, and that the sweet gravity of your manner, and the total absence of straining, bring you perhaps nearer to the latter than to the former. But these circumstances of distinction are very great, and have gladdened many besides me. Please pardon this intrusion upon your privacy. I would not have ventured to address you thus, if I had not reason to believe that you are, remotely it may be, a fellow-countryman of mine. Am I wrong in supposing that you derive your second name from the Isle of Man? You published some time ago, in the *Liverpool Mercury*, a tale of Manx life, which much interested me, and served rather to justify my conjecture.

'I am a Manxman, with a root in Cumbria, and am passionately fond of both countries; consequently I am, in some sort, made to be one of your most sympathetic readers.

'It is possible you may have read a book of mine called *Fo'c's'le Yarns* in which I have tried to tell a few Manx stories. If, as is indeed more probable, my little venture has not come under your notice, I would esteem it an honour if you would allow me to send you a copy. My object, however, in writing to you now, is to assure you of my warm admiration and sympathy. The mention of my

8-2

own book you will, I trust, regard as an attempt to produce credentials of my aptness to feel the good will which I have tried to express.'

If this letter indicated a breadth of sympathy that was apt to lose itself in generosity, I will quote again to show that Brown could be a very severe as well as a very appreciative critic. When I began to lay the keel for my first Manx craft, my first serious Manx novel, I sent a scenario to the author of *Fo'c's'le Yarns*, and this is part of his reply:

'Thanks for this admission to the secrets of your workshop. The story is most interesting. I think it best to return the sketch, as it may be convenient for purposes of reference.

'It could not possibly be placed in the Isle of Man nor timed in the nineteenth century.

'The Isle of Man does not give you the remoteness of place which you want. Norway might, Kamtschatka might! But the Isle of Man—no.

'Then as to time—

'The history of the Isle of Man since the Revestment (1765?) is not legendary, nor has it been otherwise than very clearly defined since the Reformation. It is an eventless history, but quite ascertained, and rigid within its narrow compass. The constitution has been singularly unbroken; there is not the faintest hint of any such revolution as you postulate. The House of Keys was co-optative in my own time, and the change to the popular method of election was the merest migration "from the blue bed to the brown".

'The stage is inadequate for your romance; and moreover it is quite occupied by the most obstinate fixtures. Your dooiney (*sic*) Mooar is less than a fable. Where can you get him in? He is not, I suppose, the Earl of Derby, or the Duke of Athol; but, if he is not, he ought to be; for these gentlemen hold the field, and you can't get rid of them. It is impossible to conceive the privileged class, or nobles, of whom you speak. The fact is, you would take the Isle of Man as the merest physical basis, and construct upon it a whole system of manners, institutions—a social system, in short, which it never knew. It can't be done at the distance; it can't be done at all.

'Now, why not cut away your socio-politico-revolutionary setting altogether, and rely, as no doubt you desire to do, on the sheer humanities? The Dooiney Mooar need not be a Lear, but he might be an old Manx gentleman; and instead of resigning a seigniority, he might resign his landed estate. Such a person, and grouped around him nearly all the rest of your story, you could place about the year 1800. The Duke of Athol held a sort of court in those days: he brought over with him to the island a choice assortment of swash-bucklers, and captains and miscellaneous blackguards.... This Athol episode is, I think, capable of treatment; but it brings us perilously near our own time. Bishop Wilson was an "epoch-making" personage. The Church and State question was then prominent. He was a complicated man, or at any rate a composite one. Never was man more beloved, never was there a serener saint, never a more brutal tyrant. But why seek this sort of person in the Isle of Man? Think of Laud and his tremendous stage. Has anyone ever "done" him, and the robin coming into his study, and "all to that"?

'But yours is a Romance? Not an unconditioned Romance, though, I suppose? Your sketch as related to a background is more like a Fiction founded upon fiction; or, to express it nautically, Fiction-by-fiction-half-fiction-with-a-little-bit-of-fiction.'

An opinion like that was not to be gainsaid, so I went to work again, getting a little closer to Manx soil, though still conscious that my theme was floating over the real Isle of Man as over an island of Prospero that had the interest and perhaps the charm without the responsibilities of an actual country. In this second effort I had the constant assistance of my correspondent; and when at length my work was done the best reward that came to me was the whole-hearted enthusiasm with which my first Manx novel was received by the brilliant Manxman.

'I have broken a finger and can hardly guide a pen', he wrote, 'but I must write at least a scratch or two to tell you of the delight with which I have read the new book....'

Five or six pages in Brown's minute and delicate hand of just and searching criticism, coupled with splendid if extravagant praise, are followed by this characteristic passage:

'I do so rejoice in that stark atmosphere—grey, grim, almost colourless; the very style is IN OUTLINE; no fat paint, no prettiness, no ornament—dark silver, dark STEEL, if you like. Mind, I would not have you overdo this; your sentences are just on the point of becoming jerky; they are rigid, but you must not let them become abrupt, snapped off by the keenness of their own internal tension. It is extraordinary how whole passages of this book affect me as beautiful frostwork; the icicles seem to ring in the thin air.

'But I do like this: partly it is a νέμεσις, i.e. I have a savage sort of exultation in the thought that to you our Island is not a mere fairy scene of the "lovely" and the "sweet" and the "really you know such a charming little place", such ferns, such mosses— positively demmee a little paradise of primaeval simplicity, not incapable of Lawn Tennis!

'Lord God! What a reception for the Edwins and Angelinas, this cold stern rebuke of yours. But to the συνετοί, to those who know, what comfort, what ghostly consolation in this DOURNESS! Why, there is not even a picnic, is there?'

It is hard for me to hold my hand in quoting from Brown's letters, of which I have and treasure a large number; and if I have already gone too far in reproducing my own glorification, I ask my readers to believe that of all the rewards that have come to me for my books the most precious by far has been the fact that certain of them were clasped to the breast of the man of genius who wrote *Fo'c's'le Yarns*.

Rossetti alone excepted, Brown was the most charming and brilliant creature I have ever known. 'Half sailor, half parson', as W. E. Henley happily described him, of medium height (say 5 feet

8 inches), broadly and even stolidly built, giving at first sight little
impression of the student and much of the man of the open air, with
a roll in his walk, and a sort of lurch in his talk, too, with a square
jaw, a moist and glistening eye, a mouth that could be as firm as if
cast in bronze, and then as soft as if blown in foam; strong, yet
tender, full of the joy of life, delighting in the mere sense of being
alive, loving the mountains and the sea and the sky and the song
of birds, but humanity above everything, and woman above all—
he was a man, and I think a great one.

So unusual a mixture of saint and, let me say, sinner, of scholar
and poet and parson and ordinary human frame I have never met
in any other being. He was capable of the highest flights of the
spirit when it is alone with God and feels the knitting together of
the riven tissues, the dew of Hermon, the balm of Gilead; but there
was no sanctimoniousness about Brown; no mawkish religiosity. He
loved to adjust his ideas to the rugged level of everyday life, to tune
his talk to the common *lingua vulgaris* (with an occasional 'Damn it
all, man'), whatever conventions might be made to bleed. No
affectation ever touched him, no pretence, no humbug of any kind.
As a poet he had the fulness of maternal delight in all that came up
from the depths of his being, and as a man he had the never-failing
joy of his masculinity.

He was Vice-Principal of Clifton College when I knew him first,
and when he retired from his post he made his home in the Isle of
Man. With no material interest in the welfare and prosperity of his
native Island, with few (how few!) intellectual associates there,
parting from the friends and ways of life of thirty years, nevertheless
when the burden of his work was done he returned to the Isle of
Man because he loved it, because it was linked with the tenderest
memories of his childhood and the fondest recollections of his youth;
because the graves of his kindred were there, and he had heard the
mysterious call that comes to a man's heart from the soil that gave
him birth.

I suppose there was a sense in which I too had heard it, for shortly after Brown went back to the Island I also returned to it. And then—though there was so great a difference between us—difference of age, character, and attainments—we became the closest friends, the most constant companions. We tramped the glens and climbed the hills together; and Brown would lie on the heather for sheer love of the odour of the earth and plunge in the 'dubs' of cool water that tumbled and roared in the deafening caverns of the rocks.

Five years only were given him to indulge his great love of home, yet how much he got into them! How he spent himself for the Manx people, without a thought of himself! If only a handful of his countrymen called to him he came at their bidding. He was at everybody's service, everybody's command. Distance was as nothing even to his failing strength, time as nothing, labour as nothing; and the penalties he paid he did not count.

Sometimes his friends have thought that the Island did not appreciate all this, did not realise it to the full, did not rightly apprehend the sacrifices that were being made, or the generous disproportion of the man to the work which he allowed himself to do, but there can be no question of that kind now. Manxmen and Manx women know to-day that the Island had in Brown the greatest man who was ever born to it, the finest brain, the noblest heart, the largest nature that we can yet call Manx. We do not point to his scholarship merely, though that was splendid, or to the place he won in life, though it was high and distinguished; or yet to his books, though they were full of the fire of genius and racy of the soil he loved the best. None of these answer entirely to the idea we have of the man we knew and loved so well. But the bright and brilliant soul, so strong, so humorous, so tender, so easily touched to sympathy, so gloriously gifted, so beautifully unselfish—this is the idea that answers to our memory of the first of Manxmen in the present age or any other.

I saw him last at my own house at Greeba on a day in 1897 when

I was about to leave home for a long visit to Rome, and I think he had walked across the mountains (no unusual adventure) to bid me good-bye. His health had been failing for some time, and he was rather silent, and I thought sad. My publisher was staying with me at the time, and when at length Brown, by some excuse, had drawn me out of the house on to the lawn, and we had sat down on the grass together, or, lying on it, had leaned on our elbows, he told me in a rather troubled voice what he had come to say.

'I don't want to frighten or distress you, but I want you to know...I am afraid I shall not be here when you come back.'

He would die soon. He felt it. He knew it. He was not going to make any fuss about it. Life had on the whole been worth living and he was content.

I was startled but not altogether surprised, for I too had foreseen what was coming. But I pretended that I could not take his warning seriously, so I tried to rally him—to say that he wanted a change; another visit to Clifton, or perhaps to London; the concerts at the Albert Hall, the operas at Covent Garden, and he would come back a new man. I should have known better. For months I had seen the signs of failing health and creeping age—the drooping gait, the altered size. But Brown was not to be deceived, and a little later, eye to eye, and with a long handclasp, we parted. It was a sad parting.

A few days afterwards I set out for Italy and the last letter I wrote before leaving home was written to him, saying, 'Good-bye, and God bless you', and such other words of farewell as one sends to one's friend on the eve of a long journey. But he was to take the longer journey of the two, and I had got no farther than Paris when four lines in the *Figaro*—meagre in their details, full of errors, but only too obviously authentic—told me that Brown was dead.

It was a terrible shock—that sharp asundering. I felt then, and I feel now, that with Brown's death something of myself died too, the better part of myself. I had leaned on him as on an elder brother, a wiser, stronger, purer, serener soul, to whom I could go at any time for solace and counsel and support. I did nothing without consulting him, and took no serious step without his sanction. My stories were told to him first, and he was always aware of my plans and intentions. If I have done anything which deserves to be remembered, it is only myself can know how much of what is good in it is but a reflection from the light of his splendid genius. He was to me the subtlest of appreciators, the most enthusiastic of readers, the most encouraging of critics, the most loyal of friends. To my moods of depression he brought the buoyancy of his big heart, so full of hope and courage; sustaining me amid the despondency of failure as well as the rarer, but no less real, despondency of success.

Looking back upon what I have written in these pages I see that in my anxiety to show how deep was my own indebtedness to Brown, I have omitted the more important matter of a hundred little points of personality which must be necessary to enable the reader who never knew him to gain some idea of the man as he lived.

Despite Henley's happy description of Brown as 'half sailor, half parson' it could never have been said of him that either in dress or manner, or yet in speech (save in certain hilarious moments) he let himself down in the latter character. In spite of the wind and the breath of the sea (rarely of the sanctuary) which seemed to be constantly about him, he was always the parson in appearance, in his long black coat, buttoned up close to his neck, and the thin strip of spotless white collar across his throat.

So clad you might find him in his study before breakfast in the early morning, reading Aeschylus in Dindorf's *Poetae Scenici Graeci*, or meet him in the evening striding with slow steps along the path of the precipitous cliff-head, while singing some great psalm and swinging his stick over his shoulder, as his brother Hugh used to swing his umbrella. His voice was a rich baritone, deepening to bass, and his greeting for his friend on the road was

a cheery shout. It could not be said of him that he was a good talker
in the Johnsonian, still less the Coleridgian style of prolonged mono-
logue, which led up from point to point in logical sequence until the
whole subject seemed to be covered, and there was nothing left to
say. Nor yet in the sense of the talker who starts conversation and
then sustains it by give and take. But in swift and brilliant little
sallies, and sudden and illuminating phrases (generally humorous),
he was without an equal known to me. At table one day when the
talk turned on Edward Irving, and his system of Church government, I began to say, 'I met an "Angel" once...', whereupon
Brown cut in with, 'Of course you did, and then you married
her'.

Brown was a wonderful listener too, and never seemed to betray,
under any trial of the interminable bore, the weariness of the flesh.
'Do you see this old parson coming along?' he said one day when
we were walking on the road. 'As sure as fate his first word will be
about his bad health, and he will keep me on that subject for the
next half hour.' It was so, and Brown stood it like a lamb. But
Brown was a better judge of character than of disease, for the old
parson died almost immediately afterwards.

Brown was a quick and pungent wit, and although his thrust
sometimes struck deep it never gave the impression of wounding
or rankling, and certainly it never made me say to myself, as the
wit of others has done, when it has scored at the expense of inflicting
pain: 'That was a mighty fine thing to say, old friend, but it would
have been a mighty finer thing *not* to have said it'.

Brown was a mimic of the first order. If you shut your eyes you
heard his victim's voice; if you opened them you saw his face. He
loved best to mimic his friends, even his dearest friends, and if it
ever occurred to you to whisper to yourself, 'It will be your turn
next', you generally answered (if you were a Manxman), 'Lerr'm!
He'll do no harm anyway'. When one day a member of his family
took him to task for mimicking a good old Manx Archdeacon (Moore)

to his very face he replied, 'Goodness me, woman, why shouldn't I mimic him? I love the man!'

Brown was not, in my judgment, the best of story-tellers. I have known many an old fisherman who seemed to me better at a yarn. Certainly he knew nothing about *motif* and cared little about the 'tragic mischief'. 'Look into your own heart', he would say to me, 'and let everything else go hang.' I am sure he could never have become a novelist—certainly not of the order of story-teller that has lately won the plaudits of the public without condescending to tell a story. But in the type of short story told over a pipe, which ends with a phrase, preferably a humorous phrase, Brown had no master. He made such stories as fast as he could speak. He improvised them constantly. You could see them coming. And he did not care a rush whether they told against himself or not. One such story, true or apocryphal, was of a clerical assembly of sorts which in his young days as a clergyman he had attended in Douglas. The meeting had been held in a well-known hotel, and the reverend brethren had strengthened themselves at intervals with a pipe, and perhaps a spot of spirits for their stomachs' sake. Consequently they had sat late, and when they had broken up in the early morning the streets of Douglas had been empty and silent, and before Brown, with two or three of his clerical colleagues, had gone far towards their lodgings they had found that they had lost their way. In this predicament they had been standing in the middle of the main street of Brown's native town, laughing loudly at their ridiculous situation, and perhaps suspecting the cause of it, when a rugged old sailor man, a little tipsy, had come bearing down on them. Brown had tackled him immediately. Did he know the way to so and so? Of course he did. 'You go along the way you're going until you come to the next street on the right, then you take the first on the left, then the next to the right again until you come to a public-house (shut up now, mind ye) and then....' The reverend brethren had begun to titter; whereupon the sailor man stopped, cocked his weather eye up at

Brown, and said, 'But look here, young feller, I'm on a bit of a spree myself to-night, so I don't mind going along with ye'.

Brown was a superb letter-writer. I am not ignorant of epistolary literature when I give it as my considered opinion that he was, perhaps, the last of the great letter-writers. Unlike some of us who are more or less known to the public and find pleasure in receiving letters of appreciation from strangers, but shrink from the difficult and delicate task of replying to them, Brown really loved letter-writing, and the difficulty of saying the right word to the people who praised his books was as nothing to the grace of his courtesy and the play of his humour. Anybody who called to him under a penny postage stamp was sure of an answer if it was only behind a ha'penny one. I calculate that during his last five years in the Isle of Man he may have written at least a thousand letters. The diminishing company of his intimate friends must have large numbers, unless they have been so foolish as to destroy them, not realising that while some were unimportant and perhaps trivial, others were marked for immortality. I find that Brown's letters to me were not fewer than one hundred and fifty, some of them comparatively brief, many of them lengthy, not a few very long, and of priceless value. Such knowledge, such wisdom, such infinite variety of subject and word, and above all such humanity! I should count it among the best of the good gifts of Providence if certain of them could be published: but that can never be by me, or during my lifetime.

In like manner I would give half of everything I have to be sure that Brown was always a good critic. But perhaps he was too good a man to be that, or at least too liable to be swayed by personal feelings. If the public was applauding you, you ran a serious risk of his sarcasm (rarely used, yet the most scorching I have ever known except his brother's); but you stood a good chance of his praise if you could not sell your books. There were exceptions to that rule, but not many. When one of my friends wrote a tender, if rather too intimate memoir of his mother, Brown said in his haste that it was

indelicate mush which might be sweet in a child, but of which a *man*
ought to be ashamed. When another of them wrote a novel that
became greatly popular about a farm girl and her fall, he said, 'The
poor old chap might never have been inside a farmyard in his life'.
And when a lady of my acquaintance became famous for stories on
religious subjects he said, 'All the same I wish the old girl would
drop her blessed religion and give us a bit of humanity'. No, Brown
was by no means an infallible critic; but then who is or ever has been,
from Coleridge or Goethe downwards? The age-worn highway of
literary history is strewn with the dead bones of the verdicts which
Time has reversed. The only peculiarity about Brown as a critic (he
was constantly writing reviews for Henley in the *Scots Observer*) was
that when you proved to him that he was wrong, and that his censure
had its roots in error or prejudice, he loved to be found out, and
rarely failed to make amends. He never kept his knife in the wrong
man long, being too big-hearted to do deliberate harm to anybody.

Brown was a sincere lover of humanity in almost every condition.
He could accommodate himself to any kind of company, for to his
pure heart and free mind there was nothing common or unclean.
I knew him for nearly six years before he left Clifton on his return
to the Isle of Man, and during that time he spent about six weeks of
his summer holidays at Keswick where at the same period I had a
home. Once I got him invited to the annual dinner at a public-house
of a club of Cumberland anglers, consisting for the most part of
farmers and farm labourers and one courageous curate. Brown joined
us with glee, and the strongest recollection I have of the event is of
the fine old Greek scholar standing on a stool at midnight, singing
'D'ye ken John Peel' at the top of his lusty voice.

In later days when we had both returned to the Isle of Man (where
he had arranged for me the purchase of the house in which I have
since spent so many eventful years), I asked him to one of my
robustious fishermen's suppers in the Sailors' Shelter at Peel, and
my last recollection of that event is of Brown in his spotless clerical

clothes, perched on an improvised platform, which rested precariously on a line of herring barrels on their sides, leading the company (in lieu of a speech which he refused to make) in the chorus of an old Anglo-Manx song, which consisted of one word only and sounded like the quack of a hundred ducks in a farmyard on Sunday morning when the girls of the farm are allowed an extra half hour's sleep.

Brown's love of the Isle of Man and of her people (notwithstanding certain trials of his temper) lasted to the end. He knew Man in both senses. In spite of the fun he got out of it (a fun that sometimes cost him dear, since his countrymen could not always see that what he loved most he oftenest laughed at), his love of his Island was at certain moments little short of a sacred passion. In our earliest days together in Cumberland I found myself wondering how it came to pass that he spent so many of his summer holidays in Lakeland and so few of them in the Isle of Man, but it did not take long to realise that his devotion to his native Island never failed. He was a great walker, especially on the mountains, the higher the better, and joining him nearly every other day on these excursions I could not but see that his steps led him oftenest to the stern fells on the south-west, overlooking Wastdale, from whose peaks a ghostly glimpse could be had on a clear day of our 'Lil Islan'' lying like a dove on the grey waters to the west. He was twenty-two years older than I, but he was always the first to reach the summit; and coming up to him at length I would find him standing erect with hands clasped in front of him and his face looking steadfastly forward, silent, sometimes with moist eyes, and saying, as if to himself in a half whisper, 'There she is, God bless her!'

During our last summer in Cumberland we went from Keswick to the Grasmere sports by the stage coach—Brown and his two young daughters, my young wife and myself. It was a doleful day, raining continuously while we were going down to the dale, and then leaving us to waddle in wet grass when we got there. Brown must have had some of the Viking blood mixed with his Manx, for he seemed to take a fierce joy in the bouts of wrestling in which two stalwart dalesmen, clasped together, arm to arm, and neck to neck held the earth with feet that were like the hoofs of oxen, until one or other, stripped naked to the waist, tossed his adversary over his shoulder and laid him on his back.

To my tamer spirit the tumultuous sports were of an interest less absorbing, but the drawbacks of the day at Grasmere were more than made up for by the joy of the journey back. Our coach, which was of the knife-board variety, was brought out and dried down and its six champing horses were backed into their traces and then we climbed into our seats—Brown in front by the side of the coachman, myself immediately behind, and our girls, in the general scramble for places, scattered about among strangers at the back. The rain had ceased by this time, and the sun was dipping behind the hills on the westward side of the Dummail Raise. We had a long two hours' drive before us, with nothing to enliven us but our bugle as we went clattering through the cobbled villages on the way; so, seeing that Brown was still in high spirits I set him going on the task he liked the best—that of telling Manx stories (true or nearly true), in the Anglo-Manx dialect. Then out they came, bubbling and boiling and frothing, old and new, the wild whimsical extravaganzas—the old parson in the Ramsey coach; the mothers gathering up their children like chickens when the time had come to put them to bed; the old wife nagging her old husband for selling their pig too cheap at the fair and then drinking the price of it on his way home. What joy, what delight, what delirium! How we screamed with laughter and rocked and reeled on our knife-boards, friends and strangers alike, while we drove under the heights of Helvellyn ('the last to parley with the setting sun') and then, in the gathering night, along the echoing road by the purple walls of Thirlmere, across the dark mouth of the Vale of St John, and up the steep hill to Castlerigg. Never had we heard the like of it! It was Brown at his highest, and next day I find myself asking if the best of him had ever got itself into his books.

But the deepest thing in Brown, as I knew him during the last eleven years of his life, was not his rollicking humour, coming up from his apparently unquenchable high spirits, but his pathos, his solemnity, his sentiment, which was destitute of the slightest trace of sentimentality, as the word appears to be understood in our own rather cynical age. I thought I had seen from the first that it was only in the lowlands that the humour in his talk was at 'concert pitch', and that during his rambles on the mountains, on 'the high places', his conversation had a gravity that was little short of religious exaltation.

One day we were resting half way up a Cumberland fell, with our backs to the peak and our faces to the dale, when he told me something of the bitterness of his experiences as a servitor at the University. How he had got himself to any University at all was something of a mystery to me, knowing that he had been the sixth of ten children of a poor Manx parson, who had lived chiefly on his parish tithes, and that his elder brother by seven years had first faced life as a land surveyor's apprentice on the smallest of salaries. Nevertheless, at nineteen Brown had been admitted to ChristChurch with the remission of a substantial proportion of his fees on condition that he became a servitor—did certain menial work in return, including that of waiting on the Fellows and commoners at table. What a sequel!

After this lapse of time I dare not charge my memory with the exact words he used, but I well remember the bitter ring in his voice, the stiff set of his lips, and the steely glint of his eyes as he spoke of the humiliation of his position, and of the sense of degradation he had suffered at the personal liberties of nincompoops of a higher breed who as scholars had not been fit to wipe his boots.

Yet worse came later. When at twenty-three he took his Double First and so swept nine-tenths of his tormentors off the slate, he suffered a yet deeper mortification from their superiors, for some official busybodies discovered that there was no precedent for one who had been a servitor being elected as a student! It had been a shocking piece of cruelty, and the first night after his Double First had been, he said, one of the most miserable of his life. I still see his mouth hard as bronze, as he told the story, and remember how I said to myself, 'This infamous bit of red tape has left a scar on the man's soul, and it will last as long as he lives'. It did.

Another, but tenderer if more tragic, proof of the inner solemnity which in my judgment was the deepest thing in Brown was the account he gave me on one of our mountain rambles of the death of his boy Braddan. He had been only seven years of age. Such a manly little fellow! Very gentle but very bold, wise beyond his years, strong for justice, a little king in the family, exercising (as his sister Dora has said in this book, and Brown too in one of his poems) a kind of judgeship and rulership combined over both of his younger sisters, six and four—he had been the joy of his father's heart, and the hope of his life. Then suddenly he had been smitten down by a serious disease—scarlet fever I think. It had been at once a terrible blow and the cause of a fearful dilemma. Brown's House lodged many of the Clifton boys, and he had to face his duty to them, to their parents, and to the School. The diagnosis was unmistakable; the fearful malady had begun to show, and the end seemed sure; but if I am to give an absolutely truthful record of the impression Brown's narrative left on my memory, I must say that when, late at night, the temperature had risen dangerously high, and a few hours might have settled everything one way or other, the decision of the School authorities, or the public health authorities, or whomsoever it was who determined the issue, that the boy should be removed from his father's house to the hospital immediately, had seemed to Brown to be little less than cold-blooded sentence of death. Nevertheless, with a struggle of body and soul, he had wrapped his little son in a thick blanket, carried him downstairs to the carriage at the door, and delivered him at the hospital. The next day (I think it was the next) the child was dead. This was another of the dark passages in Brown's life that drove him up to the silence and solitude of the fells, and made a great spiritual solemnity the deepest thing in his character.

Other stories which Brown told me during our rambles on the mountains served to show that his natural character was so far from answering to the accepted notion of him as 'a jolly good fellow' (save in certain hilarious moments when he was perhaps trying to escape from himself) that it was not only serious but tragic, and the finest things he had written had come up from that secret well of domestic experience where a man's suffering may be sharper than the serpent's tooth. But this is not the time to repeat such stories and I am not the man. Sufficient to the lover of Brown to know they were there.

I have only one other recollection of Brown that seems proper to this place, and that concerns the death of his wife. She died at Clifton during the early years of our friendship, and on the morning after her death he wrote to me (and no doubt to other friends) to tell of his loss. It was the most heartbreaking letter I had ever read. I read it once only, and it is little likely that I shall ever read it again, so hard is it to look upon the riven heart of a great soul in its uttermost sorrow. She had gone—she who had been his—his only—all the way up from her beautiful girlhood, when she had left father and mother and trusted herself utterly to him. In sunshine and shadow, in sorrow and joy, in dark days and fair, in success and failure—his companion, his comrade, his wife! Ah, if he had only known how much she had been to him—known it and remembered it always— every day and all day—*and if he had only told her*. . . .

'If your case is like mine don't forget to tell her. Never forget it—never! People may talk of inadequacy—but tell her. If you love her—tell her, tell her. . . . You may think she knows it already— but tell her—tell her!'

Such was Brown. And to think I have survived him by more than thirty years! My friend, my brother. HALL CAINE

VII

BROWN: A YOUNG MAN'S FRIEND
by
THE REV. EDWARD C. PATON

In 1892 began for me those five golden years when T. E. B. admitted me to his friendship, and I can never think of those years as past and over, but as years that live on in the present and grow in value the older I grow. His friends have written much about his genius for friendship and what that friendship meant, but I have never ceased to wonder that I was allowed to share that friendship with them with something added—very intimate and sacred. A young cleric is often dogmatic and self-opinionated and apt at times to become an insufferable bore—not one whom you would think would appeal to T. E. B.; but it seemed to make no difference, and he welcomed me into that happy circle of his friends. I have sometimes had an uneasy feeling that I presumed upon his kindness and that I must often have bored him; but that feeling could never last in his presence; he burnt it up in the warmth of his welcome. He made you feel he did appreciate your friendship. And it was not only his courtesy. He did understand—he did welcome and enjoy your visit. I do not think he was bored. That was the secret of his power. Nothing seemed alien or distasteful to him. His large heart took in all and loved all. Even the mean and hypocritical, one felt, were not altogether outside him. He could hate their actions and pour upon them his scorn and contempt; but running through his indignation and scorn there was something that was deeper and stronger even than pity. And he understood them. It was almost as if he felt he had a part in that evil.

> The ebb and the flow
> Of all men's hearts went through and through him.

Joined to this large-hearted sympathy—indeed, in consequence of it—was his beautiful courtesy. Beautiful is the word to describe the exquisite sensitiveness that led him to avoid hurting his friends' feelings and always to say and do the right thing to put you at your ease. Occasionally I have been present with some of his old friends when they discussed subjects of which I knew nothing. I was quite content to listen and learn, but Tom Brown, with his innate courtesy, would not let me feel I was an outsider. He would draw me into that inner circle. It was not by changing the subject of conversation, but by making me take a part in the discussion. And here his genius came in. He would not let you make a fool of yourself by talking on a subject about which you knew nothing. He had a way of suggesting a thought to you and drawing it out. And then, having put you at your ease, he might leave you alone. But even then he would address a remark to you, and look to you for confirmation as if you were his equal. I never knew him to fail in courtesy, even in little ways. I remember telling him a story that he had told me some time previously. He gave no hint that he had heard it before, and when it suddenly struck me that he had told it to me, he smilingly said, 'Yes, but you told it very well. I must remember how you worked up to the point'. That may have been so, for you could not have enjoyed Brown's company without learning how to tell a story.

His kindness put him at the mercy of anyone who required his help. He was ready at all times to preach, lecture or write. Every month he wrote a long article for the Parish Magazine. He even got up entertainments for the parish and on two occasions he arranged a series of 'Manx Scenes', for which he wrote songs. Nothing pleased him better than to welcome you to his home, from which you were released sore with laughing. His store of good stories was inexhaustible. He had the gift of digging his yarn out of dull and unpromising material, polishing it and presenting it, a perfect gem, to you.

It has been said, 'No one ever really knew Brown'. He never

fully revealed himself; but I think to some of his friends he revealed something intimate. He was so versatile and many-sided that everyone found in him just the thing that appealed to them. That is why, though he talked to me on many subjects, we not infrequently had theological discussions. I do not suppose you could call T. E. B. a theologian, and yet I know he helped me more than any man to understand some points in theology. He made the dry bones live. Of course there were subjects we never touched on, such as transubstantiation or questions of ritual and ceremonial, and I can see now how cleverly he evaded these subjects.

Though I clung to my orthodox position, my views were modified and broadened by him. Not that what Brown said to me was really unorthodox, for much of what he taught me is held by the orthodox theologians of to-day. I remember, for instance, a long discussion on 'Original Sin'; and when a year or two ago, I was reading N. P. Williams' Bampton Lectures on that subject, I almost shouted with excitement when I read in passage after passage much that Brown had told me.

A friend once said of Brown that 'he seemed in possession of some great secret of Nature which he was not free to impart to us'. That may be true, but to take one of his favourite walks with him was an inspiration and an education. He helped you to see something of the living soul of Nature. To him Nature was alive with the life of God, and he made you see. To him every flower, every blade of grass was a sacrament. He loved the spring-time best, but autumn had its message for him too. If it filled him with sadness, it was with a sadness that thrilled him and made him strong. It was

> joy diviner,
> Joy echoing in a minor,
> Joy vibrant to its pole,
> That seems but sad.

He saw in the apparent death of things, not failure, decay and death, but the endless struggle upwards—not the death struggle but the birth pangs, Nature labouring to attain her true life.

He was a true optimist and full of the joy of life. His optimism was grounded on his unshaken trust in God. Nothing he saw in Nature, nothing he saw in human life, could shake that brave confidence. His friends saw in him in spite of his joyousness and high spirits a hidden well of sorrow—a strange capacity for sadness. Mr Irwin wrote of him, 'I have never known a man with so wide an intellectual range, or of such infinite brightness who could be so deeply saddened by his own sympathies—sympathies reaching far back into his own past, or extended to present trouble, ever so remote from himself'.

I think they misunderstood the meaning of this sadness, or rather its real effect on Brown. Naturally with his large heart he felt the sorrows of the world. He too had suffered much in his long life. But this sorrow did not quench his optimism—rather was it a source of strength. Going through the vale of misery, he used it for a well.

Once, when a great sorrow had come to me, he took me for a walk and spoke words that changed my outlook on life and its sorrows. In his poem on Pain he reveals the secret of his strength. Truly to him the sorrows were

>   the tension-thrills
>   Of that serene endeavour
>   Which yields to God for ever and for ever
>   The joy that is more ancient than the hills.

This was no passing fancy. It was his strong conviction. He was certain that in the sorrow we could find our joy if we had courage and faith. The act of self-giving, of sacrifice, is for us here necessarily made with pain, but with God it is all pure joy.

No doubt he had his moods. He may have been at times impatient, discouraged and rebellious. But I know he faced his sorrow and pain bravely, and at times it almost seemed as if he deliberately plunged into the sorrow, seeking the joy he knew to be there. I cannot say how much I owe to Brown and how he helped me.

To me the man was greater than his work. He so strongly

impressed his personality on me that it has lasted and grown stronger with the years.

For some time after his passing I never heard a good story without a pang that I could not tell it to him. But that is all changed. I can feel joyously as if I shared it with him. And when I stand on Maughold Head, or see the bog bean in the Curragh, I think I know what he meant in his *Epistola ad Dakyns*. Never do I feel a sorrow without feeling him by me; and I look into those brave, wise, kind eyes, and I almost hear those words that brought comfort and help to me long years ago.

EDWARD C. PATON

VIII

RECOLLECTIONS OF T. E. BROWN

by

HENRY HANBY HAY

LATE PROFESSOR OF ENGLISH LITERATURE
GIRARD COLLEGE, PHILADELPHIA

I first saw Tom Brown, mimic, poet, scholar and gentleman, in 1856 when I was about seven years old. He was then Vice-Principal of King William's College, and even my boyish ears had heard the echo of the brilliancy of his addresses, and the renown of his lectures on general literature and Manx proverbs. I remembered, or was told, that he contended with Farrar for the prize poem and had come in second. I was walking with someone, who said, 'There goes Tom Brown', and I had a vision of a smartly dressed, blonde young man with short side-whiskers, moving along with a sharp confident step, all life and energy.

At sixteen I went to America, and Brown passed from my memory, until some time in 1894 when I received from a clerical friend a copy of Brown's poems containing *Betsy Lee*. He had evidently gained a general reputation then, for my friend dwelt on his dialect poems.

I had published a book of poems some time before that, so I sent a copy of it to Brown, and received a very delightful letter speaking of my verses as 'bits of rare delight', and giving me an invitation to be his guest on my visit to the Island.

I gladly accepted his invitation. Some forty years had passed since I first saw him, and the change was startling. The foppish aspect had disappeared. As he greeted me on his threshold with his cap drawn over his forehead he looked like an elderly and sagacious Manx skipper in very good condition. It was Tom Baynes in the flesh, but when we reached his library, I quickly changed my mind. The upper part of his head was as magnificent as that of Milton or Homer, and his voice—he had many voices—was gentle and charming. In an instant we were friends, and like a perfect host he called into action my little rivulets of thought. He dropped his bucket into the well of my shallowness, I hope the water came up clear. My American stories were welcomed, and my egotism pardoned.

At table I could not help noticing that the children seemed to be awed by his presence; with the exception of one audacious boy, and he was simply ignored.

By Sunday morning he was telling me Manx stories, in rather a guarded way. Later I was to hear similar stories, hilariously told 'with the full force of the company' as the ancient stock companies used to say.

Sunday morning found the Island at its best. My host had arranged to preach at a neighbouring church, and I announced my intention of hearing him. But the divine arbiter had something to say. 'Listen to my preaching, when God's in His heaven and all's right with the world! Shut yourself in a pew and listen to theology, when you can enjoy a pocket edition of all delights bound in green and gold! Come again, and as often as you like. Now, out, into the buoyant landscape, off to Peel, taste the delicious air, and end by enjoying Hall Caine!'

I saw that the master of boys and men must be obeyed, and at all events I secured a correspondent, a friend, and also laid the trenches for many a delicious walk, three of which are ever with me. So I departed and spent the night with Caine, who was at his best and kindest.

My first night with Hall Caine, whose romances are known throughout the world, is, as Kipling says, another story, but I quite remember him saying that Tom Brown was the greatest living Manxman.

And with that great living Manxman I particularly remember a number of walks; and the moods and tenses of those walks were all different. America is the land of brilliant talkers, but no one I ever met could converse like Tom Brown. In at least two of those walks, his humour, to quote himself, was not light and buoyant. It was sad. The walk of all walks occupied two days, and was as varied as a heavy shower, followed by a gorgeous rainbow. As we started from Ramsey, he pointed to a neighbouring hill, crowned with gorse, and said, 'Some day I hope to be found at rest on that hill—out-of-doors, out-of-doors'. As this was the summer of 1896, perhaps coming events were casting their shadows. Then the rainbow came. He wanted to know about Walt Whitman, a man I had met, as I have met so many men. As a poet Brown preferred Walt Whitman to Matthew Arnold. In all he said to me that day I recognised the poet and the historian, but never the mathematician and the scientist. After the Whitman moment, he drifted to a story illustrating Manx humour or the absence of it; for according to Tom Brown, Manx humour is really unconscious. It is a thing cautious, dry and ironical, a quaint surprise, never witty, and not always intended to raise a laugh; a thing elusive, being partly a method of speaking and action, shrewd sense expressed in a smile.

As a Manx boy I knew all the wild flowers, but Brown's was more than knowledge, he had an intimate love for them; I remember he told me the only place where the white heather grew, for he had scaled all the hills.

Books then came on the carpet. He mentioned Burns and Stevenson with an unctuous delight. He had been reading a novel, called in America *The Damnation of Thereon Ware*, which held up Romanism to scorn. This he dismissed with the remark, 'that it was clever, but abominably unfair'. He spoke of the necessity of Ireland having its own Government, and deplored the attempt of American literature to imitate Addison, when there was a great new world full of wonders to depict. Then for a moment he wooed me to American stories and traits, but presently returned to his own racy delightsomeness.

What a man! with his ruddy countenance, with his healing touch which made you desire to be honest, with his power, with his many voices; it was like talking to Shakespeare; better, probably, because Shakespeare would have kept so much to himself.

By the afternoon we were at the Falcon's Nest—Gladstone's home when he stayed at Port Erin. Up to ten that night we dominated the smoking-room, where we found a well-known English barrister, who spoiled all his good stories by telling us the exact court-room and town, and what judge was on the bench, and perchance the pedigree of the crier. We gave him story for story, shot for shot, shell for shell; as we went up to bed Brown said, 'You never let a fact stand in the way of your narrative'. I said, 'Is that an accusation?' 'Not at all,' said Brown, 'I recognise you as a man and a brother.'

In the morning we were up and away. And later climbed Cronk-ny-irey-lhaa—a hill with the ever-changeful sea at its feet; and although it rained, it was the clean rain of our native land, and did not quench our patriotism, or slacken our conversation. This was Brown's favourite walk: he had designed it, and had persuaded the owners of the land to provide convenient stiles. At the top of the slope we paused and climbed into a hollow of rocks, which Tom Brown called his pulpit, and where all his friends had to preach a sermon (two minutes and a half). Here Brown's friend, Mozley, Cardinal Newman's nephew, had preached on the basis of morals, and afterwards sent him a Latin epigram. This was the last time I saw Brown, and, I understand, this was the last walk he ever made.

I have met many great men in the course of a long life but I have no hesitation in saying that Brown was the greatest *man* I ever knew. It is no reflection on his poetry or letters to say that Brown was a bigger man than any of his works. Greatest of all was he in this, that he could so naturally and easily eliminate his gifted self and take his place on the platform of any man's mind with whom he happened to be conversing. You simply had to love the man—he was so entirely lovable.

TOM BROWN'S PULPIT

Immemorem tu ne me credas illius horae
Te duce quum stabam praeruptae vertice rupis
Et convexa maris late prospeximus una.

THOMAS MOZLEY

TRANSLATION

Believe not that I have forgotten the hour,
When guided by you, we two stood together
On the verge of the cliff of the beetling rampart,
And gazed on the rounded expanse of the seascape.

HENRY HANBY HAY

Perhaps I may be pardoned for reproducing here a poem written under the emotion of learning of Brown's death.

VICTORY

In Loving Memory of Thomas Edward Brown, *who died at* Clifton, *Oct. 29, 1897.*

God gave him love, its very depth and height,
And with love sent a band of lesser worth,
The zest for music and the force called worth,
The fitting word, the phrase of rare delight,
Expressed in sudden fire, and simple might,
Earth may not judge what only Heaven can.
What though he lacked full fame; men do not fail
Who gain the thing they most desire; and he
Loved man and God, was loved by God and man.
Of Tom Brown's life and death, this is the tale—
He lived in triumph, died in victory.

In triumph, for he loved the unclipped wing
Of first intention, which is ever young;
Loved naked hearts, loved feelings rudely sung,
The single rose, the brook, the primal spring.
Loving, he shared the good of everything.

For pine and primrose filled him with their balm,
The mountains lent him ruggedness and calm.
And the waves taught him their melodious swing,
While he taught Mona—these, indeed, were joys.
And when Death came, they met as friend meets friend;
It found him redolent of flower and sod,
In racy converse with his Clifton boys,
The brave word stopped—it was a fitting end—
From the dear lads, his spirit went to God.

I loved him well. Now that my fires burn low,
I'm saying, for my pulse is beating slow,
'Oh take me, Island, to your fragrant breast,
I'm old and weary of the potent west,
I crave—for many a year too sharply strung—
The soft slow caution of the Island tongue.
Like birds that seek the sunny south, I come,
Resting 'twixt flight and flight, my singing dumb'.
It may be then that folks may gather near,
To hear the things and people I revere.
And when they weary, I shall know a way
To keep them wholly mine, for I shall say,
'I knew Tom Brown', and at his name shall spy
A waking flash in every Manxman's eye.

The man was small, and modest in his dress,
Ruddy and calm, but sturdy none the less,
The most reposeful of created men:
And yet the eyes would twinkle now and then,
And on the lips a smile was gently felt,
And, close behind repose, alertness dwelt,
And this was all the lookers-on could see.
For them he wore invisibility.
To peasants ever, to some friends it fell
To know a man without a parallel.
Science was his, the tongues and ways of yore,
But with this poet, you forgot his lore.
But never friend forgot the joy, heaven high,
Of his calm voice and soul-reflecting eye,

For cheerful counsel, welcome, warm, and kind,
Rang in the charming music of his mind;
There drolled that humour which defies the pen,
That unctuous simplesse of the Doric men.
There, Pat was racy, Sandy keen and dry,
There droned the Manxman, with his slow, thick sigh.

His Heaven was wide, it held both rich and poor.
The single-hearted, be he prince or boor,
Might enter there, and penetrate the glade
Where Wesley, Dante, and St Francis strayed.
A very ample Heaven it was! On hate
And greed and false pretence he shut the gate,
He was!—I cannot shape the mighty line—
But how he loved the Manx is yours and mine.
He worked, and toiled, abjuring fame her smile,
To win glad freedom in the lovely Isle.
He haunted lanes, and plotted stiles. He knew
Where Lady Luck the wild white heather grew,
And through the roaring winds and midnight black
He'd lead you on and never miss the track.

I often feel—let realism smile—
He made the beauty of the little Isle.
You answer, bold Barule and Maughold grey,
And Sulby with its beauty-deepening way,
And little Port St Mary, sweetly bright,
And plumy Nickerson's half-hid delight,
And Peel's red Castle and decayed romance,
Were always beautiful—perchance, perchance—
You say the tender grace of sea and shore
Have been for ages, shall be ages more.
Perchance I dream, perhaps he made us see
The things that always were, and yet to me
The glen, the mossy brook, the mountain lone,
Each has a ruling spirit of its own:
And when two mingling spirits make a whole,
The nature spirit and the poet's soul,
Then something is! there comes a spirit grace,
An atmosphere which lingers round the place.

And will he leave us utterly bereaved,
The race he loved so well?
We need him—when we needed him he came,
Though brain was weary, foot and hand were lame;
We need him more and more,
Our little race forgets the days of yore.
We need him in the wild, unravaged lane,
We need him on the mooragh and the plain,
In primrose spring, and winter bleak and brown—
Dear elder brother of us all, come down,
And guard the wilder cliff and ancient town!
Oh, friend! Oh, father! Oh, lost heart, come down!

HENRY HANBY HAY

IX

T. E. BROWN—THE PATRIOT POET

by

WILLIAM RADCLIFFE

PAST PRESIDENT OF THE LONDON
MANX SOCIETY

In any study of the character of T. E. Brown one very distinctive feature must not be forgotten—his passionate love for the Island of his birth, for his early home, and those with whom he was associated in the bond of natural affection; for his fellow Manx people, a passion so intense that through the long years of residence in England he felt the increasing desire to return to its shores. Nor was this strong feeling attributable only to his keen appreciation of the Island's natural beauties, but also to his great interest in the inhabitants, their distinctive characteristics and ways of life, their customs and ancient lore. It was his affection for the Island and ambition to serve the Manx people that led him to sacrifice his Fellowship and prospects of a brilliant career at Oxford or in the wider service of the State, and to accept the position of Vice-Principal of King William's College, Castletown, a post of comparative obscurity.

When later compelled to leave the Island to provide for the demands of his growing family, it was his passionate patriotism that inspired his song and moved him to express his soul in his dialect poetry. And yet again later when declining health compelled his retirement, it was to the Island he came to spend the last years of his life at Ramsey, though the family ties would have made it more convenient for him to live at Clifton or at Keswick. Perhaps it is in the poem entitled *Epistola ad Dakyns* Brown expresses this passion most strongly.

There were three places that contended for the throne of his affection:

> The first is by the Avon's side
> Where tall rocks flank the winding tide.

> .   .   .   .   .   .

> The next is where a hundred fells
> Stand round the Lake like sentinels.

But beautiful as these places were, and loved by him through many a year, it was in the Isle of Man that his friend would find fullest expression of his spirit:

> The next is where God keeps for me
> A little island in the sea,
> A body for my needs, that so
> I may not all unclothèd go,
> A vital instrument whereby
> I still may commune with the sky,
> When death has loosed the plaited strands
> And left me feeling for the lands.
> Even now between its simple poles
> It has the soul of all my souls.

Brown loved the first glimpse of the Island as he approached it from the sea:

> It's clad in purple mist, my land,
> In regal robe it is apparellèd,
> A crown is set upon its head
> And on its breast a golden band—
> Land, ho! land.

He admired the noble grandeur of the Island's rocky coasts; he walked along the cliffs; he loved the blue sea that washed its shores, and often plunged into its waters or rowed on its surface; while in times of storm he pondered over its mystery and power. He felt a native companionship with the mountains and climbed them in all weathers, admiring the widespread panoramas, which included not only the surrounding peaks and undulating moorlands—with

Epistola ad Dakyns

Dakyns, when I am dead,
Three places must by you be visited
Three places excellent,
where you may ponder what I meant,
And then pass on.
Three places you must visit when I'm 'gone'.

Yes! meant, not did, old friend!
For neither you nor I shall see the end,
And do the thing we wanted,
Natheless three places shall be haunted
By what of me
The earth and air
Shall spare,
And fire and sea
Let be —
Three places lonely,
Three places, Dakyns, only —
Three places when the dead heart wakens.
Three places only, Dakyns.

Facsimile of first two stanzas: date *circa* 1869

glimpses of the glens, the lowlands and the coastline—but also the nearest highlands of the neighbouring countries as well as the intervening sea.

Often he wandered over the moorlands, across miles of heather and blaeberries, and on the lower heights delighted in the perfection of Manx gorse. Still more often he penetrated the innermost recesses of the glens, with their richly wooded slopes, whose trees were festooned with ivy and filled with singing birds; entered fairyland nooks of luxuriant foliage carpeted with moss, and picked abundant primroses and honeysuckle; admired the crystal rivulets whose banks were lined with graceful ferns; stood awestruck in the presence of deep ravines cut by the rushing streams through the solid rock; was enchanted by the cascades and fountains illuminated by the sunlight; and often bathed in the refreshing pools below the waterfalls.

In the days of his retirement he discovered the exquisite beauty of the Northern Curraghs, which being within easy reach of Ramsey, thenceforward rivalled Maughold Head, Ballaglass and Glen Auldyn in his affections.

During his latter years he was extremely pleased when old friends from the mainland would accompany him on rambles, and particularly when they admired his favourite beauty spots.

But Brown equally loved the Manx people, and had a high opinion of their character and worth. He was extremely proud of the nobility and moral grandeur of the Manx parsons of his early days, and still more proud that the Island could claim such a man of science as Edward Forbes; such a preacher as his brother Hugh Stowell Brown; such a novelist as Hall Caine; or such a breed of heroes as the Peel lifeboat crew. While he admired the excellent qualities of his countrymen, he never hesitated to admit, or point out, their faults.

On the other hand, he was always ready to defend them against false charges. On one occasion an Englishman having asserted that the Manx were dishonest in business, Brown replied that the best specimens of Manxmen were to be found in the interior of the Island, where they were uncorrupted by intercourse with business men from across the water. 'A dishonest Englishman', Brown said, 'is highly favoured by Nature—he looks so honest; while a Manxman, if he is a rogue, looks like a rogue.'

There were, it must be admitted, some Manxmen whom Brown did not at all admire. He was highly indignant with those land-owners and exploiters who shut people out from places to which they were attracted by the scenery or historical associations. He even defied the Crown Seneschal when he announced that certain footpaths were to be closed on certain days, and vigorously attacked the claims of glen proprietors to charge their admission fees.

It was owing to the apathy of the residents of Ramsey that a local Footpath Defence Association was not formed under Brown's leadership—a society whose formation at the present time would prove a very valuable memorial of Brown's connection with the town.

Others of his countrymen whom he did not like were those who were ashamed of being Manx and pretended to be English; who adopted English place-names instead of the ancient Manx. These he withered up with the fire of his sarcasm and contempt, as well as those who imitated 'trippers' by singing the 'imbecilities fabricated in the London music halls'.

For the people who had introduced the tipping system he had no use. 'On the man that bestowed the first tip on Manxmen, the curse of Mylecharane', said Brown. In short, he had no sympathy with the tendency, then beginning to develop in the Island, to sacrifice every beautiful thing, whether natural or moral, on the altar of commerce.

Brown's human sympathies were such that he came to know all sorts and conditions of people living on the Island, but particularly humble folk. He knew their daily life; he knew their joys and sorrows; their tragedies and comedies. As a student of history he had a great reverence for the past, and this included the Island's past. He had a great knowledge of its mythology; its proverbs; its folklore and its dialect, derived from the ancient Manx, the loss of which language he deeply deplored.

He was always depressed by the *tholtans* (ruined homesteads) of those who had by force of circumstances been compelled to emigrate to other lands; and it always gave him joy to welcome the return of one of these exiles on a visit to his native isle.

His love of the Island made him feel that its past was worthy of study and record and that it was his duty—and he had supreme qualifications in scholarship, powers of observation and expression, for the task—to portray the age in which he lived for future generations. He believed, too, that there was a stratification of character distinctive of the Island, which he aimed at interpreting.

Brown realised that to be faithful in his interpretation of Manx character his poems must needs be written in the dialect of the people, though he was fully conscious that in adopting this medium he was shutting himself in a narrow constituency, and that the dialect would be a more or less serious stumblingblock to the ordinary English reader. He was content to appeal to the few so long as the few were of his own people. He sacrificed any hope of reward for his labour, and the chance of popularity with the English reading world which would have been his for the having. But he could hardly have expected that his fellow-countrymen would have misunderstood him, and that he might even be charged with holding up the Manx to ridicule. This absurd view was referred to with scorn by Mr A. N. Laughton, then High Bailiff of Peel, when as chairman of one of Brown's lectures he asked, 'Does anyone say that Charles Dickens held the English up to ridicule?'

A truer view has now replaced the first comments on Brown, and Manx people the world over realise how intensely he loved them, and how deep and true was his unfailing patriotism.

Perhaps I may be allowed to conclude by quoting a poem written

by Edward Priestland, a life-long friend of Brown, and published
shortly after the latter's death.

> Mourn, Mona, thy sweet singer is no more,
> Who sang because he loved! full love, full song!
> 'Twere treason for such love to paint thy sons
> As paragons of virtue; greater treason still
> To truth; such love as his could never sing
> Half truth.
>
> Yet some did love him not, because
> His love-song ran in perfect harmony,
> Because he knew subtly to interweave
> Those undertones of truth, those discord strains
> Of native coarseness with his melody,
> And dared to write the language of thy sons
> In all its nakedness of common speech.
> They loved him not because they could not grasp
> The length and breadth, and depth and height of love
> Foursquare in all its passionate embrace
> Of native life.
>
> He loved, as they do love,
> His Island's mountains, everlasting hills,
> The beauteous girdle of her azure sea,
> And all her fairness plain to common eyes,
> And all her saints, whose memory lingers still
> In Manxmen's hearts;
>
> But with an equal love
> He loved her cushags, curraghs, claddaghs, dubs,
> Her ruined tholtans, and her crazy Chalse,
> Her sinners and her saints; he loved his love,
> For better or for worse, till death did part.
> And would they know the beauty in his life,
> Their love must be like his—a perfect love.

X

THE MANX POEMS

by

THE REV. A. J. COSTAIN
HEAD MASTER OF RYDAL SCHOOL

'To sing a song shall please my countrymen!'[1] But the Manxman is
not over-easy to please; the critical faculty is so strong in him that
the home-born poet has ill work to win his laurel wreath. 'Making
fun of the Manx' is the unpardonable crime. Truth to tell, the Man
Island harbours some of the most humourless, as well as some of
the most humorous, of men: and it is not surprising that Brown has
been suspect. These poems are about Manxmen. There is humour
in them. The inference is obvious. At whose expense is the humour?
But there is all the difference in the world between humour and
ridicule. Surely we can laugh at our friends and love them not
a whit the less. During the war *Punch* launched many a shaft at the
private soldier and those who commanded him, though at that
hour we had every cause to honour the men who were the pro-
tectors of our liberties. We have no right to laugh unless we love;
else, laughter has the ugliness of malice. If that be the test, we as
Manxmen have no quarrel with Brown. He loved the race from
which he sprang, and no one has brought or done that race more
honour. The Manxman emerges from his pages 'a man to love'
and 'a man to live with'. Brown deserves well of his countrymen and we are proud to acknowledge our debt to him. We recognise in him the greatest of Manxmen, while we are not concerned
to deny that he was also a citizen of the world.

Brown's aim in his dialect poems was to write of and for his
countrymen, 'to unlock the treasures of the Island heart'. If the
tranger had ears to hear, let him hear. If he could o'erleap the

---

[1] p. 107. References are to 'Collected Poems', ed. 1901.

barrier, he could roam at will and find pasturage. And I would bear witness in passing to the many lovers of Brown whom I have found among the Gentiles, men who leap with joy at the mere mention of his name. But it was chiefly for his own people that he wrote the *Fo'c's'le Yarns*. He felt that he was living in an age that was swiftly passing away. 'Old Manx is waning, She's dying in the thol-than.' Was he not right? She is now all but dead, a concern for scholars and antiquaries, and the English invasion has transformed the face of the land. The Douglas Quay no longer knows the little packet-boats of old. The *Ellan Vannin* was lost one black night, the *Peveril* and *Fenella* (how she lived on!) are no more, and their successors bring invaders in their thousands. Brown saw the 'tide of Empire' flooding in and wiping out the old landmarks. His was a courageous and loving attempt to enshrine the spirit of a dying age, to catch an accent that was doomed to fade.

From the very nature of the task he was forced to write in dialect. In one sense this was not natural to him; it was not the lingo of his childhood, for, as he says somewhere in his letters, he had the misfortune of belonging to the professional class. His father wrote and spoke like an English scholar, and his mother was a Scot of the borders. He tells us how his brother, Hugh Stowell Brown, who became a famous preacher—you can see his statue in Liverpool with his back to the Baptist Chapel and his face to the Philharmonic, which is a parable—missed the Keltic strain altogether. Old John, the chosen companion of his boyhood, was a dour old Scot. Brown went early to King William's College, and, after his years at Christ Church, the Island knew him no more in his working days save as a visitor with a slight taint of the 'come-over' on him. In the normal course Brown would have passed more and more out of the orbit of Manx ways and ideas, and nourished only a quietly sentimental interest in the land of his birth. His ways were set in the English countryside beside the loveliness of the Avon Gorge, and his speech was that of the cultured Englishman. Though Brown could write nervous and polished English, as his letters testify, and was a linguist deeply read in the literatures of Europe, the tongue most dear to him was the vernacular of his own Island with its quaint idiom. He slipped easily into it. He was a born mimic, and yet it was hardly mimicry, for Tom Baynes was his *alter ego*. One can imagine that it was with a sigh of relief that he launched out on the *Fo'c's'le Yarns*. He had never been convention-ridden, but all his working life he had worn the garb of a parson and the gown of a schoolmaster. He may well have wanted to shake himself free. It may be contended that he was only adopting a barbarous dialect that itself was bound to fetter him anew, but he was at least escaping from Bristol to Barrule; he was paying his tribute to the soil that had nurtured him. After all, dialect there must be, if the true flavour and savour were to be there; an intimate view of Manx life and a portrayal of Manx character only thus become possible. And no one is found to deny that Brown uses the dialect with consummate skill; though, if he had been accustomed to speak Manx Gaelic, no doubt there would have been more of the old speech embedded in the stories. Anglo-Manx is easier to understand than most dialects. A glossary is by no means as necessary in reading Brown as, say, in reading Burns, in some of whose poems word after word is foreign to the man not born in the Lowlands, while in the whole of *Betsy Lee* the editors have only given us equivalents for one hundred and three words or phrases. This would imply that in a minute's talk only one word unknown to an Englishman would occur, though there would be many a turn of phrase that had the authentic Manx tang about it. What I can recollect of fishermen's talk would confirm the truth of this proportion. It was fascinating as a page of the *Yarns*, and not a minute would pass without something said as only a Manxman could say it, but the Gaelic was ' 'lowanced'.

Brown's great achievement is that his pages are full of men and women who are alive. You feel that they are not puppets dancing at the poet's whim, but men and women, real, individual, purposeful, going their own way, with the springs of action within them—Tom Baynes, and Pazon Gale, and Cain of Renshent, and Tommy Big-Eyes and Harry Creer, prince of 'dooiney-mollas'. Tom Baynes comes first, 'old salt, old rip, old friend'. He may have had thoughts beyond his station, but so had many of his kind. I have known more than one Manx carpenter working for a weekly wage who could discourse on Kant and Hegel from dusk till dawn. Why Brown gave many of his characters names that were not Manx, I do not know, but here he was surely trying to get as near to Tom Brown as he dare. Baynes is Brown in a guernsey that the brine has greyed, and he gives us Brown's philosophy of life. In *Betsy Lee* he is the principal actor, but in most of the other Yarns he simply tells us a story in which he plays only a minor and incidental part, pleading with Mary Bell,[1] and rescuing Nelly Quine,[2] and going with Jack Pentreath to interview the Pazon.[3] He tells his story as a Manxman would, with many a shrewd hit and many a stroke of worldly wisdom.

> Pride, eh? Turn your back, and Pride
> 'll ate all you'll give him, and more beside.[4]

Or

> But still for all, if you want to catch
> Young love asleep, you must lift the latch
> Middling aisy, I tell ye, for sure,
> And not go kicking at the door:
> And if you want ta take a bird, my son,
> Alive for its beauty, no call for a gun;
> And snowdrops isn' op'nin' with puttin'
> A candle to them, nor neither shuttin';
> And the brightest brass is the better for ilin'
> And never no egg wasn' hatched with bilin'.[5]

Or

> ...bless me the way them women knows
> What's up, in a general way—when you're sick—
> And also about young gels and the lek—

---

1 *The Doctor.*   2 *Tommy Big-Eyes.*   3 *The Manx Witch.*
4 p. 300.   5 p. 198.

> It's terrible in the world, it is:
> For if two craythurs have took a kiss
> Anywhere by day or night,
> Every ould woman'll know it straight.[1]

Often you can see him nodding or shaking his head as he rolls his phrases over and over on his tongue, repeating not his more striking phrases, as is the way of an Englishman, but those that are more commonplace, as Manxmen will—'never, never', 'that's it, that's it', 'all right, all right', 'go on, go on', 'you'll get lave, you'll get lave'. When he is at the joints of his story, he is never satisfied with saying a thing once. Once interrupt him and he is a slow starter; he is apt to stay over-long in low gear, and thus slow down the narrative.

Another characteristic of Tom Baynes as a story-teller is his tendency to wander down a by-path. At any moment he is liable to digress, say, on Sailors' Homes[2] or Bach's Fugues[3] or pictures of the Madonna.[4] Occasionally you may resent the interpolation (a tribute, surely, to the interest of the main story), but you must allow that the yarn gains in verisimilitude. That is the way stories are told, and the Manxman, in particular, has a genius for parenthesis. I have heard an old Manx preacher tell four stories concurrently, with the stories winding in and out of one another with the complexity of a Ciceronian period. Some of the most characteristic passages in the *Yarns* occur in these digressions. To take an example that we could hardly omit, there is—

> Now the beauty of the thing when childher plays is
> The terrible wonderful length the days is.
> Up you jumps and out in the sun;
> And you fancy the day will never be done;
> And you're chasin' the bumbees hummin' so cross
> In the hot sweet air among the goss,

1 p. 171.   2 p. 142.   3 p. 267.   4 p. 186.

> Or gath'rin' bluebells or lookin' for eggs,
> Or peltin' the ducks with their yalla legs,
> Or a climbin' and nearly breakin' your skulls,
> Or a shoutin' for divilment after the gulls,
> Or a thinkin' of nothin', but down at the tide
> Singin' out for the happy you feel inside.
> That's the way with the kids, you know,
> And the years do come and the years do go,
> And when you look back it's all like a puff,
> Happy and over and short enough.[1]

These are lines that have been set to music and are known to many who are not familiar with Brown, but the lines that precede them are just as memorable. Brown never got nearer to linking sound and sense; you can hear the patter of little feet on the shore.

> Ah! it wouldn' be bad for some of us
> If we'd never gone furder and never fared wuss;...
> If we were skippin' and scamp'rin' and cap'rin' still
> On the sand that lies below the hill,
> Crunchin' its gray ribs with the beat
> Of our little patterin' naked feet:
> If we'd just kept childher upon the shore
> For ever and ever and ever more.[1]

He will digress about pumps, that roar like broken-winded horses—about feet, and their various angles and methods of progression—about Sailors' Homes that are prison-like in comparison with the homeliness and the discretion that obtain at Mawther Higgins' house, 'clane but not partickiler'—about cows 'with the butter meltin' in their big eyes' and the placidity of the men who tend them—about fugues that 'duck and dodge and dive and dip' like an urchin running from his mother until at last you hear the father's heavy feet 'soundin' like thunder on the street'. There are marks of close and keen observation in every line of these passages, and often an exuberant humour that sweeps story-teller and listener off their feet, unless the listener is one of those unamiable men who refuse to be amused. The humour is often enough of the riotous order,[1] though there are frequent subtle asides that evoke a smile rather than laughter.

> Aw soft, no doubt; and stupid rather;
> And takin' mos'ly after the father.[2]

We can gather from Tom Baynes and his comments something of Brown's views on man and life. He felt that life was a school of character, and character was best formed when there was a certain hardness in the process—'hard if you like; but the world is hard'.

> I believe the Pazon knew what he was at;
> I believe he knew it was good for us,
> For me and for them, for better for wuss,
> That all we had in us should have fair play,
> And all give account at the judgment day.
> Aw, the heat of young blood is a terrible thing,
> And it swims in your head, and it makes it sing
> Queer songs enough—but doesn't it loose
> Your soul, like a bud that's sticky with juice,
> Till it creaks, and it cracks, and it opens free
> In the eye of the sun most gloriously?
> Anyway—look at the other surt
> A steppin' their tippy-toes over the dirt!
> Bless ye, keepin' no company
> But only with the top of the tree;
> And no spunk in them, and no chance if they had it,
> And—marry a fortin, and be a credit![3]

With kid gloves Baynes—and may we say Brown?—had no sympathy; he preferred virility to gentility. 'Misther Richard Taylor Esqueer' was naturally enough no friend of his, and when you meet '*Misther* Harry Combe' the title rouses unjustified suspicion. 'Strong and bold and free', 'more beef than butter,

1 Cf. the milking scene, p. 121.   2 p. 377.   3 p. 157.

more lean than lard'[1]—that was what man was meant to be, and the process of education was a difficult one when the raw material was a Tommy Big-Eyes.

We can all be grateful to Brown for the gracious figure of Pazon Gale who moves through the *Yarns* like a benediction. There were parsons of another sort, as Brown knew full well. He was not ecclesiastically minded, and for the 'machine-made touch-me-nots', so prim and perfect that the devil daren't come near them, he had little liking.

> And they never done wrong
> And they never done right...ding dong, ding dong.[2]

Pazon Gale was not of that order; he was 'simple and lovin' and wise'.

> For his heart was just four pieces joined,
> A man and a woman and a child, and a kind
> Of a sort of Holy Ghost.[3]

He was a man of few words, but those words were 'meat for a hungry heart'. It is worthy of notice that Brown does not make even the Pazon a plaster saint. His very gentleness was apt to make him defer an unpleasant task. He was Manxman enough to put off till to-morrow what had been better done to-day, and was he altogether blameless for the tragedy of his home-life? But you only love him the more for not being the mirror of perfection. See him comforting the Doctor; see him in the cart beside Mary Bell, sharing the shame of that slow journey to Douglas; see him laying peaceful touch on the fevered spirit of Christmas Rose; and you have indeed the picture of a man of God. There are touches of humour again here, as he pulls manfully at a pipe that is his master, or is tricked

---

1 Cf. p. 156:

> Like trees, that grows in the open air,
> Eh, lads? and chances it, rain or fair,
> Blow high, blow low, they've got the grain
> In their heart that will polish again and again.

2 p. 587.   3 p. 157.

by the innocent wiles of Nessy Brew;[1] after all, you never know where you have a woman, and she was not where he thought she was.

Several of the *Yarns* give us Brown's picture of the Manx girl. Betsy Lee, Nelly Quine, Nessy Brew, Kitty of the Sherragh Vane—all alike are charming, and charming, we must confess, very much in the same way. *Job the White* opens with a description of English girls seen through Manx spectacles, girls who don't know 'a teat from a tail'—

> Who can't bile a priddha, and can't make a puddin',
> And knowin' nothin', excep' what they shud'n'.[2]

Per contra, the Manx girl was serviceable and 'without capers'. Nelly Quine has, to my mind, more individuality than the others. The story of her reaction to Tommy's clumsy love-making is told with real insight. She could join with the rest in baiting Tommy; but when they were alone she was an elf whose vagaries brought Tommy more uneasiness and distress than all the bullies and all the schoolmasters in the world could cause him. The whole story of *Tommy Big-Eyes* bears reading over and over again. Look, for instance, at the village school when Tommy's hen, a love token, escapes from the basket. You can see the schoolmaster improving the occasion; there are few occasions that a schoolmaster does not feel capable of improving. Encouraged by the cunningly sympathetic laughter of the school, eager as ever for any diversion, he lashes Tommy unmercifully with his tongue, and not with his tongue alone. (There ought to be a law confining schoolmasters to one weapon at a time.) Nelly being what she was sought to comfort Tommy with a kiss, and, Tommy being what he was, she could only make contact with the back of his head!

The older Manx women do not come out so well. There are a number of odious women in the *Yarns*—snobbish, grasping, jealous, full of petty meannesses, 'hardly fit'. They are not good

1 pp. 511–517.   2 p. 593.

to look upon or to listen to, for they are uncomely and their gossip has a malicious flavour. It would be a mistake to regard this as Brown's verdict on Manx women. One of his letters should reassure us on that point.

Unutterably precious to me is the woman, the native of the hills, almost my own age, or a little younger, whose spirit is set upon the finest springs, and her sympathies have an almost masculine depth, and a length of reflection that wins your confidence and stays your sinking heart. The lady can't do it. This class, of what I suppose you would call peasant woman (I won't have the word), seems made for the purpose of rectifying everything, and redressing the balance, inspiring us with that awe which the immediate presence of absolute womanhood creates in us. The plain, practical woman, with the outspoken throat and the eternal eyes. Oh, mince me, madam, mince me your pretty mincings! Deliberate your dainty reticences! Balbutient loveliness, avaunt! Here is a woman that talks like a bugle, and, in everything, sees God.[1]

Still, Mrs Lee and Mrs Baynes, Mrs Gale and Mrs Quine are unlovely and ungracious. They are not of one pattern—Tom's mother is very different from Betsy's—but they are distinctly unpleasant.

> And 'Misthress Baynes! now! was he prepared?'
> 'God knows!' says she—Aw, the woman was hard.

This emphasis on the dark side may be set down to the exigencies of story-telling. If all were fair and lovely there would be no tales to tell. Newspapers and novels would never be written if all God's children wore the shoes of angels.

The worst character in the *Yarns*, after all, is a man—Cain of Renshent whose wife is in great contrast to him; 'Wasn' she a Shimmin of Ballarat?' To be in her presence was to breathe the atmosphere of peace. Cain, her husband, was a man who under a veneer of pietism nourished an evil heart. One of the most dramatic passages in the *Yarns* is Cain's soliloquy when he was in

---

[1] *Letters,* 1, 233.

the grip of his unholy passion and he began to see himself as he was. There are some stirrings of conscience, just a faint flickering of a lamp half-lit that is doomed to extinction in the gathering storm. Even Cain had his moment, but it swiftly passed and he went to his own place.[1]

Outside the *Yarns* there is much to interest the Manx reader, and much that shows Brown's skill in portraying his countrymen. *Chalse a Killey* enshrines the memory of one to whom every farm-house door on the Island was open. Often I have heard my mother tell stories of him, and I could wish that Brown himself had heard one or two of them. With what loving insight Brown depicts him!

> While your soul,
> Dear Chalse! was dark
> As an o'erwaned moon from pole to pole,
> Yet had you still an arc
> Forlorn, a silvery rim
> Of the same light wherein the cherubim
> Bathe their glad brows.[2]

Of all Brown's poems I could least spare *Chalse a Killey*; to read it is to love the man who wrote it, and to begin to understand the man of whom it was written.

Then there is *Jus' the shy*, most genuinely Manx of all the poems. Have you ever seen the clans gather on the Colby bridge at chapel-time on a Sunday evening? 'And there wasn' a one of us went'. There is *The Pazons* with its perfervid invective and its unexpected *dénouement*—an excellent piece of fooling. And there is *Mater Dolorosa*. Henley's praise of this poem, unmeasured though it may seem, is not a whit overdone. Brown has pierced to the very heart of this stricken woman. He sees her smiling through her tears, comforting herself and her man with brave words, and then sinking to the very depths of grief as the sense of her loss comes flooding over her again. She struggles bravely, but she is in deep

---

1 pp. 307–8.   2 p. 15.

waters. How deep they were, the man who wrote *Aber Stations* knew full well. The poignancy of the closing lines is almost intolerable. With true poetic instinct Brown makes her discard the name 'Billy'; it was not big enough to convey the heart-break of the last line.

> O Illiam, the sweet it'd be to die.[1]

If Brown's first interest was in human nature, he was also passionately devoted to nature. He loved every stick and stone of the Island. The rock-bound coast, 'dark purple peaks against the sun', the shadowy glens, the murmuring streams, the scent of gorse, the cries of birds on moorland and headland—all smote upon his senses and caused him infinite delight. At some moment of stress one often hears the sound of a river or the cry of a bird, in sad accompaniment or bright relief. For instance, when the Pazon is pleading with Mary Bell's tormentors, you remember how

> there wasn' a word
> For a minute may be, and all that was heard
> Was the river, cryin' down the gill.[2]

The amazing beauty of the Island had laid hold of his very soul. It would be hard to say whether he loved it more in sunshine or in storm. The Curraghs were specially dear to him. Tommy Big-Eyes found solace there, and Chalse a Killey was surely haunted by them even in the Heaven into which he strode as a son of the house.

> Through all your dreams
> Come there no gleams
> Of morning sweet and cool
> On old Barrule?
> Breathes there no breath
> Far o'er the hills of Death
> Of a soft wind that dallies
> Among the Curragh sallies—
> Shaking the perfumed gold-dust on the streams?
> Chalse, poor Chalse.[3]

1 p. 32.   2 p. 433.   3 p. 14.

He notes how cold and austere the whitewashed farmhouse looks in the grey dawn,[1] and how stunted the trees are on the windswept coast.[2] You are often made aware of the scent of honeysuckle. You hear the cows stirring in the shippon and the dogs barking on the 'street'. The sun rising out of the sea is 'the red that ript the East',[3] and if you have ever sailed into Douglas at dawn and seen the sun striking fire from every window on the long front you will know that Pazon Gale had some comfort from the beauty of the world that morning, even before he heard the lark in high heaven.[4]

The typically Manx touches are a delight. What Sassenach could feel the force of 'That's love; and thank my God it's in'? There is an infinite wealth of meaning in the preposition. Very true to life is Nessy's 'but I didn' stop' at the end of her description of the 'feer'. The whole business is dismissed with a careless gesture, effective but somewhat affected; this simulation of indifference is a Manx idiosyncrasy. 'Not that I care one spit about it', I have heard an old Manxwoman say, when she was fishing for information she would have given worlds to possess. Manx caution and the habit of understatement are often evidenced; the quality of a sermon or the condition of the crops or the state of your health is seldom better than 'middlin''. There are many passages, too, in which there is a sense of far horizons and a touch of that mysticism which is a common trait in Manx character. We catch glimpses, too, of ghos'es and fairies and big bugganes, the whole host of the 'little people' who used to haunt the Island. Delightful is the contempt shown to Adam and Eve for their folly in Eden, with the final wail—

But loss the place! loss the place!

The whole story of the courting of Nessy Brew, first by the whole pack of miner lads and afterwards by the favoured twain, is 'rael Manx'. Danny Bewildher—his proper name, of course, was Danny the Spout!—is an amusing caricature of a schoolmaster of the days when it was accounted a shameful thing for an able-bodied man to

1 p. 535.   2 p. 179.   3 p. 435.   4 p. 436.

ply such a trade. The passage on 'Knowing'[1] is very characteristic
of the type of Manxman who thinks that to repeat an assertion is
to prove it. Have you ever heard a Manxman prove that ours is the
most wonderful race in the world? The courting scene in *Betsy Lee*
is worthy of quotation at length; it takes you right into the kitchen
of a fisherman's cottage.

> Aw, them courtin' times! Well it's no use tryin'
> To tell what they were, and time is flyin'.
> But you know how it is—the father pretendin'
> He never sees nothin', and the mother mendin',
> Or a grippin' the Bible, and spellin' a tex',
> And a eyein' us now-and-then over her specs.
> Aw, they were a decent pair enough them two!
> If it was only with them I'd had to do.
> Bless me! the larned he was in the flowers!
> And how he would talk for hours and hours
> About diggin' and dungin' and weedin' and seedin',
> And sometimes a bit of a smell at the readin';
> And Betsy and me sittin' back in the chimley,
> And her a clickin' her needles so nim'ly,
> And me lookin' straight in ould Anthony's face,
> And a stealin' my arm round Betsy's wais'.
> Aw, the shy she was! But when Anthony said:
> 'Now, childher! it's time to be goin' to bed',
> Then Betsy would say, as we all of us riz:
> 'I wonder what sort of a night it is';
> Or—'Never mind, father! I'll shut the door'.
> And shut it she did, you may be sure;
> Only the way she done it, d'ye see?
> I was outside, but so was she![2]

It is generally allowed that he handled his technical problems with
great skill, though one acute critic[3] has suggested that the use of

---

1 p. 375.   2 p. 112.
3 Mr H. Percy Kelly. To him and to Mr Philip Cain and to Mr Ramsey
Moore I owe most of what is apposite in this chapter, but they are not in any
way responsible for its defects.

dialogue would have helped him not a little. In choosing to write in 'asynartete octosyllables' Brown set himself a rather difficult problem. The longer and looser line which he used in *Jus' the shy* would have given the slow-moving story-teller more room to turn round in. Alliteration is one of his favourite devices, and he is fond of strings of words of equal length—'laughin' and lovin' and livin'', 'diggin' and dungin'', 'messin' and muddin'', 'sniffin' and snuffin'', 'the sand and the spray, and the scud and the stars', 'suckin' and sobbin'', and 'retchin' and cretchin'', and 'slubbin' and slobbin''.

> And curlin' and purlin' and pippin' and poppin',
> And booin' and cooin', and stippin' and stoppin'.[1]

His rimes are sometimes forced, and he is capable of varying his spelling to help out his rimes. He is ready to make 'chokeder' rime with 'Docthor', and 'it yet' with 'idiut' and 'she was' with 'albatross'. He was more or less driven to devices of this sort. On the other hand, some rimes that look strange in print are by no means far-fetched; 'shore' and 'knew her' are quite near enough on a Manx tongue. Anti-climax is frequent, but you never have the feeling that he is unconscious of it; it is often employed with obvious intent. When Tom Baynes ends his description of Betsy Lee with

> And she stood just five feet four in her shoes,

you can imagine him getting down to solid earth again with a sigh of relief! *Kitty of the Sherragh Vane* ends with

> And I stayed to the weddin', bein' invited.

Then there was Marky the Bird (son of Jemmy Jem), melancholy, poetic, musical, and

> a lightish slaeper
> And went to the town to be a draeper.

The dialect verse is full of flashes of poetry. In the middle of a prosaic narrative you will suddenly come upon lines that contain the very stuff of poetry. If to see images is the business of a poet, who can deny Brown's claim to the august title? He gives us many a bright-gleaming figure.

> Some witch or another
> Must have spun that stuff. . .it was black as nubs
> But streaks of red, like you'll see in the dubs
> Where they're cutting the turf; or down in the river
> Where it's deeper and darker and redder than ever—
> And all like a cloud around her scutched—
> Aw, she must have been wutched, she must have been wutched.[1]

When Tommy went with his story to Mrs Cain 'he'd stumbled into an old grave'. Death is a fisherman 'who hauls you into his boat and wrenches the hooks'. The lightning is a monster licking up the sea with a tongue of fire. First Love is 'one wave flung in upon the shore, That bursts and breaks for evermore'. Whenever he describes the sea, in any of its moods, his touch is masterly. In a passage full of insight and marked by rare beauty he shows us Christmas Rose looking out upon a world in which things inexplicably strange to her were happening; no one has ever given us a more intimate picture of spiritual loneliness.[2] The metaphors and similes are rarely conventional and often homely, well suited to the character of the man telling the story.

> Haven' I tould you every word,
> To the very keel of my heart?[3]

Or (speaking of the scent of apples on the bough, sweeter far than incense)

> Like some faery was fishin'
> With a smell for a bait.[4]

Mary Bell's wanton beauty is vividly described.

> For she'd keep the eyes upon you, ye know,
> And the deep light gatherin' there as slow,
> Like tricklin' into a bowl, till she'd fill it
> Full to the brim, and then she'd spill it
> Right in your face.[5]

1 p. 161.　　2 pp. 189–191.　　3 p. 182.　　4 p. 543.　　5 p. 419.

When Katty Bell is speaking, you hear

> The sweet talk running off her lips
> Like water on an oar on the feather.[1]

Tommy Big-Eyes was 'as innocent as a biddhag bowl'.[2] The last sixty lines of *Christmas Rose*[3] show Brown rising to the height of his powers as a story-teller. The drama moves swiftly to its inevitable end, as she who came out of the storm is summoned home.

Brown stands revealed as a man with a teeming brain and a great heart. His interests were well-nigh universal. Music, art, literature, religion and philosophy were all laid under contribution. He writes now like one full of the lore of the storied past, now like a man of his hands whose care is all for the airt of the wind and for fishing-marks. He can be worldly-wise at times, but he has too the wisdom not of this world. He loved the rich red earth.

> O Mother Earth, by the bright sky above thee,
> I love thee, O, I love thee!

He was, too, a great lover of his kind. He loved men well enough to paint them as they were. The faults and foibles and follies of men were an open book to him, but they did not blind him to whatever strength and courage and beauty underlay them. These stories of men and women are so told that you begin to see your fellows with his eyes. *The Doctor* is in many ways a tragic story, but you remember how it ends—

> You liked little Katty? Well, that's enough.

Which is not to say that these are stories 'with a purpose'. They are just plain tales from the quayside, tales of Manx men and women, their loves and their hatreds, their joys, and their fair and evil deeds. Sometimes they seem to take a fuller sweep and to embrace a wider humanity than the Island holds; but that is as it should be. It was not without reason that ours was called the island of Man.

A. J. COSTAIN

1 p. 441.   2 p. 265.   3 p. 208.

XI

T. E. BROWN, 1876–1881

by

SIR HENRY NEWBOLT, C.H.

Those Cliftonians who have written about T. E. Brown are naturally the friends and pupils who knew him intimately or saw him often: but perhaps there may also be room for a word from one who had neither of these advantages and yet retains after fifty years the memory of a vital influence. In my five years at Clifton I never saw or heard Brown in a schoolroom, and I seldom had any talk with him outside —between the Modern Side and the Classical there was a wide gulf fixed. It was not till two years after I left that Brown began to lecture on English Literature to the whole Sixth Form. But it is quite certain that at all times we were all aware of his personality. He ranked among the powers who created and directed our daily life: he was one of our household gods, and of that wonderful company—all of them to us immortals—none was more reverenced or relied upon. He pervaded our life, and if he had gone away for a time we should all have known it without being told.

To begin with there was his bodily presence, in every way significant. His structure was large—large in bone rather than in bulk, but unmistakably weighty. He walked with the measured gait of a big seafaring man—Horatio Brown said excellently that 'he had a slow sort of urgent walk, like Leviathan pressing through the floods'. To me he seemed almost like the floods themselves, like deep river water, or a heavy tide ' rolling in, rolling in, rolling in upon a dead lee shore '. When you saw him enter room, field or Chapel you had the impression of an elemental force—an existence that could not know physical fatigue. His face and voice confirmed it: a grave face with broad forehead and strong prominent chin, framed completely by hair and beard, so that the mask was outlined as clearly as that of a lion. Then suddenly the set mouth would move, the leonine gaze turn human, light up kindly or indignantly, and the voice followed. Perhaps it was by that voice that we remembered him best. Mellow and rich it was always, but at times a sound to shiver at, angry or ironical: anyhow not to be forgotten. I remember a sermon in Chapel: often of course a quiet time for straying among one's own thoughts. I had left following the preacher, but was not yet far away, when I became aware that his tone was rising. A moment afterwards I was brought back to full consciousness by a huge melodious roar—'Leave your dark corners, your spiritual dens and caves! Come forth, you little moral Troglodytes, come into the daylight's splendour—There with joy your praises tender. . . .' The sound— the real joy in it—was in our ears for weeks after: the phrase 'You moral Troglodyte' became a permanent addition to our vocabulary.

Another recollection I have of his voice and manner. We had a Prize for English Verse, and in my last year I found time to compete for it—that is to say I scrambled off some hundred and twenty lines of blank verse, a lament over the fall of Athens, put into the mouth of Athene herself, who showed a creditable acquaintance with our school History of Greece. I knew that Couch would be practically my only competitor, and I was more disappointed than surprised when I heard that he had won the prize with an excellent poem in a more varied style. Brown was the judge who had made the award, and he said to me afterwards, with a kindly gleam of amusement, 'I am sorry I couldn't give you the English Verse: but you see . . . there was Couch. No matter—*he'll* be read by half a dozen, *you* by one'. I replied to the effect that that was not quite the same thing. 'Yes it is', he said, 'better: *your* audience will be unanimous'. It did not occur to me to ask if he would have accepted the same consolation himself.

But that was not because I did not know and value his poems, even then. My brother has stated, in his *Clifton College Forty Years Ago*, that 'Brown was never appreciated at School, as he is now, and will be while great poetry is read'. I remember copies of *Betsy Lee*—the only book of his, I think, then published—and we discussed it, with some differences of opinion, but certainly with appreciation. My own copy was handed about until it perished of overwork. And our interest was greatly stimulated by the enthusiasm of my House-master, Wollaston, and by the influence of Brown's fellow-Manxman, Wilson, who succeeded Percival as our Headmaster in May, 1879. At Easter in the following year I went with Wilson to the Isle of Man for a fortnight, and we walked almost all over the Island. On the voyage, which took some hours, and was windy, Wilson suggested that we should take shelter on the fo'c's'le of the ship, and there, lying on the deck, he recited to me Brown's poems in Manx dialect, hour after hour. This was not merely a great feat of memory—he can do the same to-day, after fifty years—it was an ideal presentation of a work of art—insight, accent and dramatic sympathy were all there—and I have often thought, when I have heard the dialect spoken of as a diminution of the value of these poems, that ten minutes of such recitation would never fail to bring about an exactly opposite conclusion.

My good fortune did not end there. When I returned to Clifton, where I had still a year and a half to spend, I found myself a hundred miles nearer to Brown than I had ever hoped to be. I was not an islander, but I had at any rate 'made the Island Voyage', and though Brown was the most impartial of men, the most distant touch with Kirk Braddan was in his eyes an aureole. I am sure he would have given me anything I had asked him for—except, of course, the prize that was Couch's.

HENRY NEWBOLT

A BUNDLE
OF
UNPUBLISHED LETTERS

SOME LETTERS

by

T. E. B.

HITHERTO UNPUBLISHED

Extracts of letters from T. E. B. *to his* MOTHER

ChristChurch
4 November 1850

My reason for writing so soon is the following: I have again to pay 'thirds' for the rooms I occupy this term. They amount to £15. 3. 6. This is no small sum, and although when Evans who now has my old rooms pays thirds for them I shall receive some £8 or so, yet I believe it will be necessary to pay this first. Now I have just £15. 3. 0 in my purse and no more. Accordingly after I have paid this sum (and the sooner it's done the better) I shall be completely penniless and in debt one sixpence. I therefore think it would be well if you could forward me by return of post £5 and of course you can pay yourself out of any money that may come into your hands on my account. These thirds are a very great nuisance; for although the expense is not great in the end, yet it is very inconvenient just at the time. I probably shall not spend more than £1 before Christmas, except the travelling expenses, and therefore £5 would I fancy be sufficient. I hope I may receive Evans' thirds before I go down. If I do, there would be little occasion for my receiving money from you now, except that one can't be here where paper etc. are necessary articles without a single farthing in pocket. After this botheration is got over I fancy my expenses will be next to nothing, except for travelling; and indeed, I have good hopes that there may be a decent surplus of income over expenditure at the end of the (College) year, which will be very much at your service.

ChristChurch

13 *November* 1850

I was glad to receive your letter and enclosure yesterday; the bill I have not yet got cashed, but intend doing so immediately. I am almost sorry you entrusted me with so much; for really if I am liable to be extravagant in any way, it is in the way of books, and when severely tempted, as I often am by the excellent and cheap works which one can buy here, I find it a very salutary regulation to keep as little money about me as I can. However, ten pounds will make me feel more comfortable, and I have resolved to give up all book-buying for this term. I continue to be tortured by the higher branches of mathematics, into which a wily tutor hath seduced me, and I am enjoying as heartily as ever man did the fun and frolic of Aristophanes.

6 *February* 1851

You should have heard from me before now, if it had not been that Little Go was pending, and I did not like to write before the important affair was over. I am now happy to say that all's right, and that I have passed with great ease, although not a little anxiety, for such things always put me out of the way terribly. I can now settle down to read quietly for the rest of the term, and that will be a great blessing.

I must thankfully acknowledge receipt of the £2; when it reached me I had only four shillings and sixpence in my possession, and was beginning to feel a very poor brick. I think it is almost absolutely certain that I shall receive a quarter of my exhibition this term. If so, I shall be very comfortable, and banish dull care for some time to come. I hope the parting with £2 did not cause you much inconvenience.

ChristChurch

22 *June* 1851

...Fowler told me the other day that I looked as though I fasted three times a week. The fact is I am as thin as a lath and will make a very interesting specimen of 'a mummy who died from starvation', to be presented to the library of King William's College....

I shall have to work like a brick this vacation. I shall be much pressed for time, for I happen to fall in a most unlucky year, and Stoker has just had a long consultation with me from which it appears that I am to read for First Class! It will be tremendous work for the next few years.

4 *November* 1851

...Verily it is high time for me to begin thinking of sermonizing! A man's life at the University, however it may be calculated to store his head with knowledge, is scarcely the thing to strengthen his hands for action. We travel over so much ground that we have scarcely time to mark the favourable positions and commanding heights which it affords for the practical work of the battle of life. Perhaps it is best to work out the course thoroughly as it is, and then I shall have more chance of having some time to look about me before I buckle on my armour and set to work in right earnest....

I go quietly working on, steadily keeping the end in view. The poem, however, is in progress, and with the help of such inspiration as I may catch on the old shores of our Isle during the vacation I hope to bring it up here next term complete. As far as it goes I rather feel satisfied; but when it is finished I shall submit it to the opinion of competent judges, Stoker among the rest, though there are some undergraduates here whose opinion in such matters I should prefer to that of the whole Hebdomadal Board.

ChristChurch

7 November 1852

...Today there is a thorough roaring of the wind that does my heart good. I can't bear that deadness of nature which is the general characteristic of English county scenery. I like the stir and commotion of the storm. It does instead of the beating of the sea. I am working somewhat harder than usual; and as the subjects are quite congenial, I take great pleasure in my studies.

8, Barton Street, Gloucester

11 *May* 1862

I am now conscious of 32, and on the whole I think I feel it. But considering the year of bother I have passed through, I don't think I am amiss after all.

A very good instance of the sort of bother I am subject to in my exalted position as Headmaster of a place like this, was brought under my notice this morning. The other day I called a nasty, lazy, ill-mannered young whelp at the school 'a little hog'. Today I received a letter from the father demanding an explanation!!! Can absurdity go further? However, I am becoming gradually very thick-skinned. Twelve months ago this foolery would have annoyed me. At present I can laugh at it.

2 June 1862

...Notwithstanding all our difficulties, Marshall and I have resolved to work the ship fairly into port. Accordingly we are going on with the work until Monday, or at the latest Wednesday, when we hope to have the prizes down from London, and to distribute them. If we can do this we shall of course break up the same day. I preach at Oxford on Whit Tuesday.

Extracts of letters from T. E. B. *to his sister* MARGARET
(*afterwards* MRS WILLIAMSON)

ChristChurch

4 April 1853

It is now a long time since I received your last letter, and I am to blame for not answering it before this; but truly I have plenty to do at present, and little time for anything but my studies. This morning, however, I have heard from Mamma, and she tells me that you are very unwell. You can't conceive how much this disturbs and distresses me. But I do hope that it is nothing very serious, and that it will shortly pass away and leave you as jolly as ever. Surely you have been working too hard, cramming (like me) for your great go—eh? You mustn't overdo the thing you know; I can tell from my own experience how injurious that is.

Shouldn't you like to 'pur a sight' on the Isle of Man again? I'm sure it would do you good. The very sight of the old mountains, the breath of the old sea, would refresh you. Your vacation is now not very far off, I suppose: but still it might be better to knock off at once, and retire, not as Neddy Creech hath it, 'quite abashed' but a little done up, that's all. I hope this summer to bring Alfred down from London with me; so that we shall be quite the old circle again, and we must try and enjoy ourselves as best we may. If you are determined to study, I shall be very happy to take you as a partner through a quadrille consisting imprimis of a course of modern history and politics, second, of English and international law!! What say you? A pleasant prospect, forsooth! Well, it might be worse, as witness my present labours in the *ancient* world. I will tell you what, you must teach me German and I'll teach you Latin or some old bogey, whichever you like, provided it is within the compass of my accomplishments. Music, everlasting blessed music, will of course engage

some of our attention, and Annie Laurie will excuse us if we sometimes maltreat her a little, for, as saith Mr Traddles, she is such a dear
girl, that one likes to romp with her a little. Can you sketch from
nature? That is one thing I am most anxious to learn. By 'nature'
I mean, for instance, a sketch of Castletown market place with old
Parsons, round, rich and ventricose in the foreground, and a choice
collection of the most remarkable oddities (including perhaps my
humble self) in the background. A fine subject, if we only knew
how to treat it!!

I have just been thinking over a plan. Considering that your
health is so delicate, I think it would not be right for you to go to
work at anything in the governess way at least for some time,
certainly not till you are quite strong and healthy again. Well, there's
one point. Now I am likely to be ordained to some place in the
Isle of Man about Xtmas next, and shall probably have a house
and shall want a housekeeper. Now takin' these two premisses
into consideration, what is more obvious than the conclusion that,
if you pleased to accept the distinguished preferment, you might
even become said housekeeper. I know the honour is great, and the
position one of immense importance and dignity!! Still don't allow
this to deter you; but think of it favourably if you can!!! I think
you and I should get on very jollily: I should be as cross as a beast
sometimes you know; but I won't strike you; upon my word I won't;
and won't grumble about hashed mutton and cold potatoes or anything of that sort, and as for white-chokers, why you mustn't put
too much starch into them, that's all, for a very stiff choker is
enough to try the temper of any man. Then if you got tired of me
and my old bachelor ways, why you might migrate you know; but
indeed you shouldn't, unless the Bachelor aforesaid had good reason
to suppose that you were 'rough and tough and up to snuff enough'
to work at something else. Now what do you think? If you feel
well enough to write, do let me know your opinion. Fancy the
young curate (who would be 'really an angel, if it wasn't for the

pimples') and his interesting sister—why it's 'wergin on the poetical'
I declare.

I don't know where the place may be, but that wouldn't matter
much, would it? Provided it's within those eighty miles of rock-
bound circuit y'cleped the waste of Mona it's sure to be pleasant
and not far from the mountains or the sea, our best old friends.

I really quite enjoy the prospect. But I can fancy you expostulating,
'But, Tom, how can all this be when you're engaged?' My heye!
Who put that note into your head; and if I am, what matter! If ever
the engagee, you know, comes to see me, you can give her a cup of
tea, can't you? You needn't fight or make disagreeable faces at one
another, need you? Why, bless my heart! what's 'the use o' talkin'?
I shall (possibly) be in the Isle of Man within 6 or 8 weeks. The
Examination is on in about 3 weeks. I'm rather funky, not of a
pluck you may suppose. But then people do form such extravagant
expectations of a poor fellow; not only people in the I. of Man, but
here too, expectations which I know I can't fulfil. However, the
contest will soon be over, and all decided, and verily Mr T. E. Brown
will feel slightly relieved, shake his head clear like a new day, and
away, away, away, glad to be rid of it. I'm going, however, to have
another slap at the schools next Oct.; the subjects are those which
I mentioned above as likely to be my study during the long vacation.
In Oct. I fancy I shall be here only about a fortnight. And then
farewell, a long farewell to Old Oxford! Heaven help her in her
hour of need! What she'll do without *me* I don't know!!!

But I must work, work, work. So good bye, my dear Margaret!
Mind you take care of yourself, and mind above all things that you
be as jolly and cheery as possible, and look forward, as I in all my
troubles do, to a happy meeting when 'the golden summer comes'.
With love to Harriet and all the North Country girls, including the
Irish, but not the *Welsh* (mind!), believe me

Your affectionate brother

THOS. E. BROWN

Mr T. E. Brown Fellow of Castletown Coll. somewhere between this and the North Pole. I haven't a map, or any astronomical instrument to determine the position. Goodbye.

Oriel College

24 *March* 1855

Many many thanks for your most delightful letter. You may easily imagine that the *main subject* of it alone would make it excessively interesting to me. But this was not all; for the spirit of your kind words was most fresh and luxurious to me. . . .

Pardon me if I presume to say that I knew, and knew with the most perfect and undoubting confidence that you would like Amelia; and let me add that I know now with just the same confidence that you will very soon love her. Indeed the dear delightful expressions that you use with regard to her are a sufficient guarantee for that. Amelia will be more and more loved by you the more you know her. She is quite as reserved as you can be; and it is long before anyone can learn fully to appreciate her. But depend upon it, the more intimate you become, the more wonderfully will her sweetness and gentleness be shown; and at the bottom of all you will find what transcends all, a strong and earnest goodness, a kind of happy facility of always thinking aright on every subject, a kind of impossibility of ever erring intentionally, which must come from God; for nothing so good comes from any other source. I never beheld anything like this. I am sure if you knew all it would amaze you— the wonderful clearness with which through the most complicated case of conflicting beauties, this earnest, unbending conviction of right enables her to see her way at once. . . . There is not a being in the world to whom I should as soon go for counsel as to her. The understanding of the wise and prudent is completely put to the blush by the simple, unpretending, unaffected truth and goodness of one little girl.

Clifton

8 *October* 1874

My plan of visiting the Island in August broke down miserably under the abominable weather....At least Amelia and I determined to be off to Switzerland. We were away about five weeks, but this only gave us less than a month in Switzerland. We were detained three brutal days at Dover. Our three weeks in Switzerland were consummate. No rain, no wind, a perpetual bath of sunshine, hot of course, but at those heights deliciously bracing and stimulating; sunshine that got into your brain and heart and set you all aglow with a sweet radiant fire I never thought possible for my old jaded *apparatus physicus*. We went by Paris to Neuf Châtel; thence to Berne, Interlaken, Lauterbrunnen, Mürren. Here we stayed a week. It was the best part of our holiday. A week never never to be forgotten. Mürren faces the Jungfrau. The glorious creature is your one object of interest from morning to night. It seems so near that you could fancy a stone might be thrown across to it. Between you and it is a broad valley, but so deep and the sides so precipitous that it is entirely out of sight. So the Jungfrau vis-à-vises you frankly through the bright sweet intervening air. And then she has such moods, such unutterable smiles, such inscrutable sulks; such growls of rage suppressed; such thunder of avalanches; such crowns of stars! One evening our sunset was the real *ecstasis*.

11 *December* 1878

I have unfortunately lost your letter or I would have replied before now. I have been much harassed. One of our boys after a ten days' illness has died. It was measles, followed by inflammation of the lungs. He was a nice gentle little creature. We have been fearfully worried by these measles. Our own children have had them before;

and thank God are just now especially well. And it is grand weather to be well in. How exquisite the hoar-frost is on the down! Every branch a coral, every stalk of grass a feather of diamonds. But our little friend lies at the Sanatorium, stiff and cold, and almost as beautiful as they.

I tell you plainly, Margaret, I don't know what to do or think. These things will not lose their terror for me; and in the presence of them my soul is a chaos. It is not that I fear; it is merely that I am dead, and inconceivably miserable. I seem to make no progress; I get neither hard nor elastic—crash they come into my very heart, these balls, riddle me through and through, leave me an almost ludicrous object. I can organize no defence; the next shot will find me just the same; a poor old battered target on Death's Rifle Range—and oh that awful marker who crawls from his hut and squints at me and scores!

This is the way I go on from year to year. I know that these things must come at all but regular intervals, and during these intervals I am fain to get what happiness I can. But how uncertain it all is!...

T. E. BROWN

Hotel Minerva, Rome

10 *January* 1880

I have been here about a fortnight, and shall be for a week more. Two of our masters accompany me and we are a jolly party. We have a little salon to ourselves, with grand wood fire, smoke like factory chimneys, and work hard at this enormous palimpsest of a city. There is Rome beneath Rome, and Rome beneath that again, a sort of three-decker of archaeology. To go straight down from one to the other at various points is easy enough; but to reconstruct them all and several so as thoroughly to realise their mutual inclusion and exclusion is a work of endless patience, of ceaseless confusion, of repentance, amendment, re-repentance, and oftentimes final despair. One might be content with Rome as it is. In which case—there you are; Blue and gold atmosphere all day long and every day; No cloud, no breath of wind, warm sun, or oranges and lemons ripening and ripe in the garden, moths like gorgeous gourds basking in the sun; beggars with elaborate lizards sneaking in the sun, peasant women and Roman women lovely for colour, peasant men with goatskin breeches and marvellous intricacies of nondescript raiment, grinning in the sun—but everywhere sun, sun, sun! Splendid shops; splendid equipages; a great band playing in the brilliant entourage of promenaders on the Pincian—German students in red gowns, other students in black and purple, others in black and blue, others in black and green—St Peter's opposite glowing in the last blaze of the aforesaid sun. Funerals in the street, long processions of hooded mourners, then white-laced surpliced clergy, then blessed little boys also in white lace and black petticoats, then the crucifix, then more priests and boys, and then, borne by four hooded figures with faces quite concealed, the essential element of the proceeding; and often the body of some very poor person about whom all this ceremony is scrupulously, and it would seem reverentially and fraternally, observed. Churches with their great heavy leather curtains in front of the doors, into which if you enter, you will feel the soft sweet puff of the incense, and see upon their knees here and there, scattered like flowers in the pleasant irregularity of a meadow, motherly creatures, with their babies, every one a study for a Madonna, and every one praying like the mischief. Galleries of statues and pictures where are gathered up in a central world's heart the *absolute* treasures. Are we to thank the Popes, or are we not? Accidentally—was it that they did all this—not for use? Though we gain the advantage? At any rate here they are—the Vatican Apollo, the Sleeping Ariadne and a thousand more.

The Vatican, take my word for it, is as far beyond all other collections as Lincoln Cathedral is beyond—say St Barnabas Church,

Douglas. Not only (though this is the chief matter) are the works of art quite unapproachable, but they are so superbly housed and erected.

So I ramble on, and entirely omit Ancient Rome, my oldest friend, the unquestioned, confidant of my childish imaginings.—The Rome of Cicero, of Pompey, and of Caracalla. But I must not bore you longer. Let me at any rate wish you and John a very Happy New Year—a wish wished under the very shadow of the Pantheon and therefore auspicious surely; Better, sincere and from my inmost heart.

Clifton College, Bristol

13 *December* 1882

We are in the very thick of examinations. With boils and seeths around us, and the sky is black....I am still very lame. I suffered very much all September, October and November, being a complete cripple and having a great wound unhealed in my ankle. So I took heart of grace and went up to London. I saw Prescott Hewett; and low and behold he pronounced my trouble to be mainly gout!!! Not the real thing though—no—there would have been some credit in that—but goutiness determining to a weak point like the spring.... I can now get into school, but I can't kneel or take any liberties....

Have you or John read much of Galt? If not—especially if you have not read 'The Annals of a Parish'—may I send you my copy? He absolutely enchants me. It is West Scotland (Ayrshire) but divine. What a genius!...If I am asked for a specimen of the peculiar delicacy of touch that I find in Galt, let me give you this—Perpend it well. 'And so she died at Hallowe'en, which caused many to remark it was strange she should die on Hallowe'en.' Isn't it supreme? Note the 'caused'—the delicious senile tenuity of the argument from cause to effect. Note the repetition of 'on Hallowe'en', not even 'on sic a nicht' but rigidly, unsparingly (you'll not be let off a word) 'on Hallowe'en'. But this is a trifle. The work is all one splendour of gentlest, loveablest, limited horizon——limited! God bless these limitations! At the end of them, and that very close, He is Himself, of a truth...; and I don't want to pass beyond. D— all telescopes!...Scotland is very rich in these 'harvests of a quiet eye'. Strange too, seeing the race is so keen and fiery.

Ventnor, Isle of Wight

12 *January* 1885

...In June I took to a wild scheme of bathing in the Bristol Channel. I used to rush off about 6 p.m. and bathe far down the coast, and rush back by train just in time for bed. This very soon knocked me up. I was in a queer way; the doctors shook their heads and hinted at paralysis. This was absurd; however they had me off to the I. of Man. This was not absurd but delightful! Fancy all July in the Isle of Man! At Ramsey! With strict injunctions to be quiet!!! I stayed down with the aunts. I had some boating; but mainly I walked backwards and forwards on a platform of sandhills carpeted with bluebells, which was just above the house. Did a few proprieties! Finally I climbed Barrule, and having thus satisfied myself that I was all right, I crossed to Keswick. Here we had a glorious time, mountain climbing unlimited. I returned to Clifton in September like a giant refreshed with sundry wines, and I have been very well ever since.

Penmaenmawr

11 *August* 1886

The Carnedds are really noble mountains, and I have been tramping along the whole ridge from Tal-y-fan by Moel Fras to Carnedd David—I delicately and carefully follow this ridge, poise myself upon a watershed 'as upon an horse', and thus escape: Very few people go up there. How delicious the mosses are! and the quartz blocks! and the singing streams! Always new to me, the blessed things! The slope Conway-wards is quite full of streams, which, high up, come gurgling through unfathomable beds of moss. The whole mountain is one sweet golden gurgle.

Clifton

17 *May* 1888

Write and tell me how John gets on. We are in a terrible plight. Amelia's illness has taken a very dangerous turn. We have been watching her now for a week day and night with the utmost anxiety; and we are nearly done. Edie and Ethel are admirable, but they will soon be off their legs and heads as well. I can't sleep. Amelia has a rooted antipathy to having a nurse. I have just smuggled one in, but she daren't show her face yet. The disease is peritonitis supervening upon, possibly caused by, the intestinal disease from which she has now so long been suffering.

All this makes me think all the more about you, and your trouble. How hard it all seems! Yet out of the bitter comes the sweet. Thank God, never in all my life did I feel more closely the certainty that all is well. The scales of a materialism, never native to my constitution, seem to fall from my eyes, and I see, dimly enough it is true, but irrefragably, the things unseen. It is only a question of degree; One day it will all go, and oh, the waking! There is no doubt about this in my mind. Death is merely the instrument of transition; nay, it is hardly even transition.

19 *May* 1888

It is coming quickly—the dark shadow. Today there has been a consultation and my darling's case is pronounced hopeless; she may live possibly a fortnight, most likely not so long.

I can't write more—we are cast down indeed, but I trust not destroyed. God give her and us the victory!

But I must not *think*!

I shall be very anxious to hear of your dear husband. How I wish, my dearest sister, you could have been with us through this trial! With us in spirit you are; but it would have been a comfort to see you and have clasped your hand.

Clifton

17 *June* 1888

I fear my last letter must have given you a shock. There was an air of abruptness about it, perhaps of impatience. But what I feel is that I must make up my mind to lose my poor darling, and the effort to assimilate this feeling and co-ordinate it with the other facts of life is a great one, and causes the jerkiness of unqualified announcement to you. It is not always, however, jerk and shock and spasmodic effort. God is dealing with me more mercifully than that, and I am at times fully resigned and can look upon it all quite calmly and composedly. May He give my poor wife a full trust and confidence which will best avail her now! Her chances of life are next to nil. She is unquestionably fading away. We get caught in the coils of language and our own words distress and even madden us, but there is no occasion for this. The thing is a *sober reality*, and ought to be faced as such. Amelia may live until the holidays, but I for one do not think so. If she does, we shall remain here; and I hope, before that, you will have got away to some nice health-giving place. Don't bracket yourself with me in a leash of misery....

Ah if I could only write something cheerful! However there is something not altogether cheerless in the thought that God has given me grace fairly to grapple with the spirits of discontent and unbelief. How he deals with *her* who shall say? He knows best, and in these long hours of quiet painless sinking I doubt not He is unfastening the moorings. I can't do that—I positively can't; but I don't think He, for a moment, needs my assistance.

Ullswater

10 *July* 1888

I came here on Saturday. It is very lovely and is doing me good. The weather is of course variable, but I do not dislike the familiar old drizzle. On Sunday afternoon I went up to Hayswater Tarn. Yesterday I walked by Grasmere, thence to Thirlspot, and up Helvellyn, so back over Striding Edge to Patterdale. I took this walk chiefly because it involved the climb up Helvellyn that we have most generally taken, and which last year revealed to me for the first time that my poor darling had lost her old activity and strength. Every step recalls some incident that revealed this; it was to me yesterday a real via dolorosa, a ladder every rung of which was a several sorrow; for I never can forgive myself for not having perceived the terrible suffering which such an ascent involved. I kissed the cold grey cairn, and I cried to her with a bitter cry. Yet thank God this is not the permanent mood. Far more usually I am blessing God and thanking Him for all the happiness He gave us, and to Her I speak of meeting again, a meeting which will not be long to wait for. It is the sweetest thought, and I have a conviction so strong that it cannot be stronger; we shall be re-united; and the old mountains know it; and, in their half humourous connivance, smile. There are very few people about, none of them I think gentle-folk. Two delightful lads from Macclesfield, not gentlemen educationally speaking; nay, one of them has an accent which makes him to me nearly unintelligible. But they are such nice fellows, the true English breed of the best kind. It is so pleasant to find that youth can have all this, and yet be quite a *ruffian*. There is sweet blood yet in the veins of this England. The lads are so absolutely unaffected, simplicity itself. Isn't that wonderful? They are well dressed, and well mannered, but their lingo is tremendous. I shall never forget the modest way in which one of them showed me a piece of staghorn moss as if it were something quite rare. 'What's yon?' he said. But 'how good and joyful a thing it is' that they should be like this, and feel and think like this. They refresh me more than I can tell.

Today I have had a quiet walk down the East side of the lake, in absolute solitude. I took the steamer back from How Town, and got a good wetting as I did yesterday, but then I got dry again, for I walked about 24 miles, and the last half the weather was fine.

How is John? and how far are you nearer to a rational sort of life? Poor Amelia! it was one of her sayings a few days before she died— 'I want to get back into the home of a human being'. I return to Clifton on Saturday, and some day the following week I shall get down to see you, if you are still in Cardiff, or somewhere near.

You can have no idea what my two girls have been to me through this trial. Fancy Edie! strong, patient, full of courage! I never saw anything like it. But she looks such a frail little thing. She and Ethel were both present when their mother died: it was an inexpressibly touching sight—the thorough sense of duty that seemed to bear them up. Edie was perfectly calm, and held Amelia's hand, till I took it and felt the last suspicion of a clasp that pulsed through those precious fingers, now so cold and motionless, and hidden away. I never before saw a person die: and, of course, to Edie and Ethel it was their first experience. To fit death into life, and this death into my life, is not the real concern. God helping me, I have no doubt but that I shall be able to do it, and to attain a lasting unity of the two—death in life, and life in death. We must not be faithless, but believing, and we must not be timid or nervous, but brave and strong.

My best love is always yours,

T. E. BROWN

Clifton

29 *November* 1891

Hall Caine is writing a story called St. Bridget's Eve. It is to appear in the Ramsey Courier and other papers. The scene is Kirk Maughold. We had a pleasant time together in the Island. Did I tell you of my reading prayers in Maughold Church? What a place! What memories! And Mr. and Mrs. White good and sweet as ever. I don't know whether the Russian tour is to come off or not. For my part I don't care for a Tendenz novel. 'Uncle Tom's Cabin' is a splendid instance, but it's not a good novel. Have I told you that I have finally arranged to surrender my House and Mastership in July 1892? The determination is my own. And if I don't surrender to the 'grim shadow' before, I may have a year or two to twiddle my thumbs. I suppose though that 63 is about my tether. It is a rum thing to meet, but it will have to be met.

T. E. B.

1 *August* 1892

We are on the eve of the departure. Did you know that I was in London having my portrait painted for the College? Richmond painted me—such fun! A tremendous talker! We got on very well together.

I must say London has still attractions for me, and I felt that after all, if I could only afford it, I had rather live there than anywhere else. However, it is settled—the I. of Man it shall be; for me probably final, but not necessarily so for the children. At my death they will be a good deal better off and they can live where they like. Meantime old Kirk Maughold will serve my turn.

Windsor Mount, Ramsey

6 September 1892

...Our house begins to look very nice and comfortable; and the broad views of leisure which open up before me are very cheering. I have been hunting up some of my old friends, such as Ballaglass. Yesterday I went up Barrule; On the way I overtook a very decent cottar, and became his guide, philosopher and friend for the day. I took him by perilous paths to the Gob ny Skute but he held out splendidly. God bless the creature! He was so pleasant, so grateful, and so MODEST.

Last night I had a treat. Did you ever hear of Tilly Bennet? She lives quite close....Miss M. is a very clever musician; so we actually had some Chopin, and very well played too.

18 September 1892

...Here it blows great guns, day and night. Wind is certainly the great drawback of the I. of Man. I remember when I was quite unconscious of its effects, and could not understand Marshall and Naylor when they complained that they could not keep their hats on their heads, hardly their heads on their shoulders. Now I am keenly sensible of the discomfort....On Friday week I crossed to Keswick and climbed some of the lesser mountains. Then to Hall Caine's, the other side of Keswick. The evening was gloomy, sad and even seedy. Yet on the hill I had the vision so dear to me, and Amelia came to me and streamed into my heart....Saturday was a delicious day. H. Caine and I walked up Borrowdale to Greenup Gill. Never did I see the place lovelier. On Monday I returned to Ramsey having a stormy passage. And now I am quite content to stay here for an indefinite time. I write, I read, I feel I am getting stronger both in body and mind. But oh ye dreadful winds, do be quiet!

Aeolus, old man! do give them the d— best hiding and lock them up in the Gob ny Skute made and 'set for that purpose'.

Love to John. Kind remembrances to your nice servant.

Ramsey

7 January 1893

I returned from Peel yesterday. My business at Peel was twofold—

1. To lecture.

2. To be at a dinner given by Hall Caine to the fishermen of Peel and their wives—no one to come who was under 60. So we were a well-matured party. On Thursday we had the lecture, a continuation of my Manx reminiscences. One more will finish them. This was 'From Rushen to Bride'. I spoke for two hours and a half. Probably you would not be unwilling to see this ragamuffin effusion. When I get a decent report of it you shall have it. Occasionally as I read it I have misgivings. I slept on Thursday night at the Graves' where I was royally entertained. Next day found me the guest of Hall Caine. The dinner came off at 7. The men had arranged everything themselves—decorations, programme and all. Poor old chaps! Their singing was terrific! I had no idea that such unmelodious ramblement could ever have commended itself to them as music. But there was so much simplicity and kindliness that one could not help being pleased. A duet by two old gentlemen was the best. They did not sing it as a duet so commonly called, but in antiphon. One man sang a verse in Manx, and the other replied with a translation in English. Well, that was the sort of thing. No public, no reporters, just ourselves. Mr. and Mrs. Hall Caine and I were the only visitors. There was a sort of understanding that no *parsons* were to be there, no *quality*. The conditions expressed were 'above 60' 'daycent' fishermen and their wives. As a successor to the Galilean fishermen who fished for a while in Gennesaret I could have claimed to pass

even this test; The 'daycent' was critical, but no one seemed to question my possession of that quality. So there I was and I carved a tremendous bit of roast meat with an abominable knife, and carved and carved and hewed and hewed—mortal carving. Then I sang two songs, also I told a short story. Cashen the assistant Harbour Master, a Dalby man, made an absolutely magnificent speech in proposing the health of Mr. and Mrs. Hall Caine. You never heard the like. No grammar, completely free and fluent, voice of thunder, exquisite felicity of topics selected and of language splendidly spurted—the man was delightful. Such a fine old fellow too! Very clever of brain and noble of heart. Then poor Hall got up and, as he himself will have it, was paralysed.

Ramsey

4 February 1893

We are quite alive here, tayparties, and the lek of yandor—treminjis! I was at one the other day and told them some made-up stories in the Anglo-Manx. 'Terble laughin' to be sure'! But I must try the other tack; If that fails I should drop the whole business. What I want to try is, whether a pathetic story told in the same tongue will make them laugh or cry. I heard a dear little bright Irishman recite 'Lord Ullin's daughter' at Cronkbourne the other day. He burst into a wild torrent of tears and sobs. They burst into fits of laughter!! Splendid little chap from Belfast—he recovered himself wonderfully and just dashed a bason of smiles over his face and went on as though nothing had happened.... You must know my Peel lecture has given great offence at Castletown....I have a good story about 'Thomas Caine'. Do you know it?—

He was christening a child; suddenly he stopped, uttered a cry of pain and began to suck his thumb. 'See', he exclaimed, 'it's blood! Yes it is, aw dear, aw dear! I'm bleedin', yes, I am; look here, good people. Why do you bring childher to be christened with pins? It's a shame and a scandal, that's what it is. Why can't you get a bit of tape and a needle?' Then a long pause and a suck. Couldn't be pacified. Made two or three starts to resume the service, but returned each time to his scowldin. At last he finished with 'Lizzen, good people, all of ye; tell everybody navar to bring babies with pins to be christened'. Then, after a long time and more or less satisfactory bloodless suck, it got christened, though, to the full.

Ramsey

9 December 1894

...I refused the Archdeaconry of the I. of Man which was offered me by Mr. Asquith. I had not applied for it, and did not want it. What I judge now above everything else is freedom, and I will not barter it for place or gold. And next I value literary leisure; I must read. God only knows the depths of my ignorance. You see the life of a schoolmaster is a perfect death unto learning. It develops certain muscles, unduly perhaps—physical and mental. But the intellect and the heart perish. Look at a dried-up snuffy toadstool! That is the 'schoolmaster of many years' standing'. What will you do with it? Well, the fact is you unconsciously, I dare say, kick it, and the fungus powder goes near to blinding you.

18 January 1895

My Douglas lecture was a ghastly failure. Such are the accidents that attend literary production. My bundle of notes would show you how absolutely I missed fire. There is scarcely a thing in them that I contrived to bring off in the lecture, and I uttered a lot of bosh which was never contemplated in my notes. Omission, commission —see General Confession in the Prayer Book! The people were most cordial and indulgent. The worst thing about them was that they laughed so much, thus stimulating me to the blankest nonsense. It is so easy to be funny; And, if you are tired, or anything puts you out, that is the most obvious, and I fear in my case the most natural, refuge.

To make the life at the vicarage amusing to grotesque! Good God! You surely don't think that was my object. But judging from the short report in the newspapers, that is the impression I get. Teach me to be cool, analytical, dry, if you like, and uninteresting; teach me not to hear the laugh that coaxes, or the cheer that inebriates; and I may do well. But as it is, the infernal demon of Buffoonery beckons at the end of every vista, and I rush into its idiot embrace and grin.

Ramsey

18 *November* 1895

...I don't care for dramatized novels, and I am quite certain that the habit of writing novels with a view to ultimate dramatization is a bad habit, and tends to spoil the novel. It makes a man strain and heave up to dramatic, i.e. theatrical, effects and sensation scenes, thus demoralizing the style and disfiguring the plot with false emphasis and glare....M. W. yes I have him; he lived close to Braddan vicarage at Ballastole gate. He was quite young, I think a baker's apprentice. In his teens I should suppose, perhaps a year or two older than I; perhaps the same age. He had begun to preach among the Wesleyans or Primitives, and was just what washerwomen would regard as a genius. But there was a sufficiently sound reality about the lad to impress me with his sincerity, and, what is more, his modesty. All this may have changed; he may have since then preached and prayed himself to rags; for it is an awful life, the Ministerial, is it not? Of dissipation and histrionic wear-and-tear, *sturm und drang*, patching, snatching, catching, all-things-to-all-men (oh, that's Paul!), affectations innumerable, affectation of sympathy along with the whole gamut of emotion and ethical tatters, affectation of simplicity, affectation of profundity. Hang it all! Put the puppets to bed, you that are their wives, and let them honestly snore. How few of them are like John Williamson. He never wore paint.

Ramsey

20 *December* 1895

...Meanwhile the people are enjoying themselves greatly. Bazaars are the principal delight. It is amusing how worldly we are all becoming. Worldly and fashionable, bless you! There's not a hair to choose between the denominations. With all my experience of modern enterprise and change of manners, I find it hard to assort my ideas to the phenomenon of a Prim. Methodist Bazaar with raffles, fortune-telling, tableaux vivants, dramatic interludes, costumes reported individually, no doubt with great satisfaction to the 'fair wearers'. I suppose the Church began these 'divilments' but they have been taken up universally and enthusiastically, and we are borne away on one big stream of pious gaiety toward what Niagara, who shall say? Puritanism is clean dead. I, for my part, am not satisfied. It may have undergone some transformation, and the spirit still be latent under these tomfooleries. It was a fine spring of life and conduct. I fear we have not been faithful, and Armida's garden lies too near the sanctuary. How do you find the spirit of your people in this matter? Urging for more concession to the spirit of the world, more amusement, display, laxity, frivolity, indulgence of youthful exuberance, subordination of the senior to the junior, enjoyment at any price? The altar turned into a Maypole, minister and deacons kicking up behind and before in truly Davidian style, reckless of their Michals? Confound this generation! England is to be assimilated to Southern Europe, not in noble art, but in childish wantonness; perhaps, too, in cunning, and the poverty of principle.

Ramsey

12 *November* 1893

Has John delivered his lecture on the Isle of Man yet? If so, do send it to me in whatever form it has appeared.

I know he loves the Island: but his intention to retire here some day must be relegated to the departments of dreams. Most delightful it would be if you both could make up your minds to take a cottage up Glen Auldhyn. There are some very nice ones not more than a mile from Ramsey, and well sheltered within the closing hills. But I suspect we shall have to think of other vales and other hills. All right, we'll have our retaliation of you. It is not a very rash speculation that gives us after death abundance of what we most loved on earth, and full capacity of enjoying that abundance. *Per contra*, hell may be the same abundance without the capacity. So heaven and hell might be not only under the same management, but positively one—a scheme which has at least the merit of being economical. The abundance of the capacity, that is the thing. Surely Elysium will not be a poor-house? Fancy having one's portions dealt out by some celestial Bumble! and being scolded like Oliver Twist when we ask for more. But I have a better opinion of—however let me pass on.

Did you ever hear or know of Mr. Egbert Rydings of Laxey? He is the man who manages St. George's Mill for Ruskin. Well, the man is a genius. It is nothing short of a miracle that he should reproduce the Anglo-Manx dialect in the way he does. He beats us all. We haven't a chance with him.

8 *December* 1893

...Delightful story of ould Anthony Lewthewaite. He was sorely tempted by the divil. The divil was trying to get him to do something perfectly awful, and he bothered him all the way down to the chapel. Directly Anthony got his finger on the chapel latch he turned upon his tempter and said, 'Theer! Theer! Go and do it theeself! Thou're fit enough for it'. And he went into the chapel and tuk a lovely prayer as comfible as comfible.

11 April 1894

I have been again up Glen Auldhyn—that is your old retreat, and the longed for sojourn of your serene or less serene moments. 'When shall our labours find an end'; under the benediction of the late lamented Paddy Criggal? Your glen is a mash of primroses and wood anemones, and on the table where I write are five bouquets of my picking, each in its several pitcher. Altogether I had four hours up there of unmixed delight. The gorse flames up abundantly, and the larches are the real emerald, now also tipped with the fresh young tassels of crimson. True, it has been thundering more or less all day; but none the worse for that. The spring is impatient and will not be kept back any longer. Hence these loud fanfares of confident victory.

Yesterday I went to the station to meet Mr. and Mrs. Hall Caine. They did not come; but instead I seized another Mr. Caine, the parish clerk of Braddan, and took him off to my house in triumph. I had made his acquaintance before at Braddan and at Arthur Moore's. A man about seventy, hale and hearty, with such a beautiful complexion and face, not unlike old Mr. Howard. We made him take dinner with us, and wasn't he proud, and wasn't he happy? He had been wanting a change, and the vicar had told him to make tracks for the north. He knew next to nothing of the north, and was like a day-old babe ready to dart off in any direction. Carpet-bag, umbrella, and a fine topper hat, he was ready for the Pole if needs were. I sent him off ultimately in a somewhat vague Boreal bee-line. I hope he hit the light-house. His desire, however, was to get lodgings at a farm house where the people lived 'in the way' he used to live himself. A truly delightful, impractical, irresponsible, dear old soul. I gave him two portraits of Father, whom he remembers well.

Ramsey

25 *November* 1894

So you are getting over your Manx longings, choking them down, or vigorously expelling them with the besom of practical working life. Aw well, you'll get lave!—But when they do become something a little less vapoury, condense into a form sufficiently apprehensible, let us hear from you! We can bide our time. What better could you do than come here and say goodbye for ever to the big country? I dare say the best thing would be to work to the last. But I imagine you are hardly game for this. A selvage, a slope, a quiet interval, and — — then. In good sooth we have not seen enough of each other all these years. I am constantly reminded of this; we are the only two, and our lives are strewn with things that ought not to be forgotten. Just now I am preparing for a lecture on old Kirk Braddan to be delivered in January. I shall give it to Douglas folk. And you may fancy how the wells spring up and flood me with memories. From time to time I miss links, and stretch out my hand ineffectually after waifs and strays, and then I would give anything to have you at my side. Nor is it merely the facts; it is the humour in which they are steeped and the emotions which they appeal to and elicit—of these you only have the secret, and all the rest is vanity. The 'county' for instance; 'Mary Corlett', 'Mary Cowle'—these are stops to turn on, voices from the earliest consciousness. You shall hear them in my lecture. Mr. Craine of Onchan, Mrs Craine—oh for one snatch of that primeval laughter! *You* can do it, you only. Then what the devil is the use of other people 'skreighin'? Couldn't you detone it into a phonograph? We should then have it conserved 'for the purposes of a life that is beyond life' (Joannis Miltonis—your pardon's asked). As I write standing at my desk I have a portrait of Hugh over against me, not many inches off. What a man! It is quite the finest of all his photographs, representing him in the very plenitude of his life and strength. Probably it dates from about his fortieth year. The hair is worn long, the beard is Newgate-fringed, chin otherwise clean shaven. The right hand is thrust into the bosom. He is stout, even inclined to be abdominal. The mouth is very richly curved, humorous, with a tendency to a possible voluptuous. Altogether a glorious fellow. Oh, for an hour with him—just as he was then! Would he have scattered my Manxmen with a noble scorn? Would he have secretly, beneath the table, grasped my Manx hand and given me assurance of the true eternal bond? Ah, well, we should have had a good time. And have you fully considered how little we have of him? Look here—shall I tell the truth about Hugh? We want a portrait—shall I make it? I sometimes think it is well within me, and that I can't much longer suppress it. My Manx book for Macmillan perhaps would give me the opportunity. I can promise you you shall have Father in it; and if that does not please you, I shall be disappointed. But I stake my reputation on the likeness. And why not Hugh? I must think about it. Hints and suggestions from you and John would be invaluable. Especially I should invite your attention to one point, viz: how to give general interest to what at first sight would seem to be a private concern. Must one begin apologetically, and so lead up to 'the height of this great argument'? Or ought one rather to assert at once and boldly the greatness of the men, proving it afterwards by elaborate presentation? I have sometimes a misgiving that we Browns make too much of ourselves. But we were, the more I think of it, an extraordinary family; and who is to know it if you and I the only survivors do not exclaim it to the world? (!!!!) And the world will laugh at us? D— it! let them; i.e. the contemporary world. But I would leave it with the utmost confidence to the future. I know what the future will think of the present, how it will stand affected to our generation. Depend upon it, the last word has not been said. A book of that sort, utterly neglected at the time it was published would lie as dead as...a chrysalis; but it would have its day, wings would lie hidden in the brittle case, and the light of a clearer air would be for it to pierce through and permeate. But a chrysalis? A butterfly? an ephemeran? Poor book! One thing is certain that I would give worlds for just such a book disinterred from the dustheap of, say, the 17th century. And is not this a natural feeling, one that we can calculate on?

But — — bless mee sowl!

Arthur Moore is going to bring out a book of Manx Songs: I am to write an Introductory Essay. There's for you now!

Love to the Chrysostoian

Ever yours,

T. E. BROWN

CONTRIBUTIONS

by

T. E. B.

to

THE CLIFTON COLLEGE
HYMN BOOK

*The numerals given are those of the enlarged
Sixth Edition of 1924*

88

88

O Jesus, Saviour, from on high
On us Thy purchased gifts bestow,
The daily-strengthening grace supply,
And let our hearts Thy presence know;
Ascended Lord, enthroned above,
Thou hast not ceased our souls to love
In heaven, as here Thou didst below.

Lord, we are weak, but Thou art strong,
Give us submission to Thy will;
Give strength that, though Thou tarry long,
We may believe Thy promise still.
Thou wilt return Thy saints to free,
To reign in Sion gloriously,
And all our long desires fulfil.

Yet, Lord, we are but feeble dust,
The ages pass, the heavens are dumb;
In Thee, in Thee is all our trust,
But death's dark chills our souls benumb;
We do not doubt, we look, we wait,
We think we hear Thee at the gate;
Lord Jesus, oh that Thou wouldst come!

Written for the tune of 'Es ist
das Heil uns kommen her'.
Wittenberg 1524.

HYMN 112

112

Now all men thank ye God
With joyful acclamations,
Who doeth wondrous things
To us and to all nations;
Who from our mother's womb
Hath blest us to this day,
Who doth all good bestow,
And keepeth us alway.

God give a joyful heart
Unto His people ever;
And may we have great peace,
Full, sure, and broken never;
That so His grace and truth
To us and to our land,
On firm foundation laid,
From age to age shall stand.

To God the Father praise
In earth and highest heaven;
And unto God the Son,
Be equal glory given;
Praise God the Holy Ghost,
The God whom we adore,
Almighty, Three in One,
Henceforth for evermore.

Translated from M. Rinckart's paraphrase of *Ecclesiasticus*, l, 22–24.
The tune is 'Nun Danket Alle Gott'.

J. Cruger 1649.

HYMN 135

135 To God alone the song we raise,
The God that will not fail us;
In vain, while He doth guard our ways,
All evil shall assail us.
God is well-pleased to be our friend,
The peace He gives shall have no end,
In His great loving-kindness.

O God the Father, Heavenly King,
Thy throne that stands unshaken,
Thy praise, Thy glory we would sing,
And joys divine awaken.
No bounds Thy power constrain, Thy will
Hath course, and is accomplish'd still;
O happy whom Thou rulest!

O one-begotten Son, in whom
Thy Father's love delighteth;
O Lamb of God, who bear'st the doom
Our sinful hearts affrighteth;
Our Lord, our God, receive the cry
Of utmost need; to Thee we fly;
In mercy, Jesu, hear us!

O Holy Ghost, O sovereign Light,
Thou Comforter all-healing,
Defend us now from Satan's might,
Thy joy, Thy truth revealing
To those whom Christ redeem'd from loss
In anguish on the bitter cross!
O great is our salvation!

Translated from the German version of *Gloria in excelsis* by N. Von Hofe (1519–41).

The tune also is possibly by Von Hofe, based on a chorale of the Latin Church. It is included in Mendelssohn's *St Paul*.

HYMN 141

141   O Love Divine, how sweet Thou art!
When shall I find my willing heart
All taken up by Thee?
My longing soul cries out to prove
The greatness of redeeming love,
The love of Christ to me.

More strong His love than death or hell;
Its riches are unsearchable;
The first-born sons of light
Desire in vain its depths to see,
They cannot reach the mystery,
The length, and breadth, and height.

Varied from Charles Wesley.
The tune is 'Nun ruhen alle Wälder'.
Heinrich Isaac (born 1440).

HYMN 173

173
Cease, my soul, thy tribulation,
Banish all thy griefs and fears;
Christ, in Whom is thy salvation,
Calls thee from the vale of tears.
From the desert where we roam
He will lead the wanderers home,
Unto joys all joys transcending,
Unto peace that knows no ending.

Light me, O Thou Star uprising,
Jesus, all my glory be;
So will I, the shame despising,
Take my cross and follow Thee.
Help me, with Thy presence blest,
Till I gain the perfect rest;
Till the grave's dark gate enfold me,
With Thy word assure, uphold me.

Trusting in Thy love so tender,
I will bear the bitter strife;
Glad to Thee my soul surrender;
Death shall be the path of life.
Thou who openedst Paradise
To the dying sinner's eyes,
Jesus, Thou wilt never leave me,
But to Thy great light receive me.

Translated from a German hymn, ascribed to S. Graf.
The tune is 'Alleluia' by Samuel Sebastian Wesley.

A BIBLIOGRAPHY

by

WILLIAM RADCLIFFE

THE PUBLICATION
OF
T. E. B.'s POEMS

Many of the poems, before appearing in book form, had already appeared anonymously in the columns of the *Isle of Man Times* or as booklets intended for private circulation. Others were published in various magazines, notably the *National Observer* and the *New Review*.

While collecting his poems, written over a lengthy period, Brown expressed some uncertainty about the unity of thought pervading them. Some of them he called 'strangers whose voices he didn't recognise'.

In 1900, three years after his death, a collected edition of Brown's poems was issued under the joint editorship of H. F. Brown, H. G. Dakyns and W. E. Henley. In 1908 a selection omitting the dialect poems was issued by Macmillan in the 'Golden Treasury Series', with an introduction by H. F. Brown. (In the *Oxford Book of English Verse*, 1900, six pages are devoted to T. E. B.)

The first edition of the *Collected Poems* contained an introduction and notes by H. F. Brown and H. G. Dakyns, the second edition an introduction by W. E. Henley, which will be found in all subsequent editions.

The volumes tabulated on the adjoining page were published in the poet's lifetime. The collected edition was made up of the volumes indicated in the first column, with the addition of some which were previously published in the *National Observer* and the *New Review*, and others never before published.

Volumes included in *Collected Poems*	Publisher	Previous editions	Remarks
(1) *Fo'c's'le Yarns including Betsy Lee and other Poems.* 2nd edition, 1889	Macmillan and Co.	1st edition, 1881	*Betsy Lee* was published in volume form by Macmillan in 1873 with no author's name
(2) *The Doctor and other Poems.* 2nd edition, 1891	Swan Sonnenschein and Co.	1st edition, 1887	In 1891 was issued a separate edition of *Kitty of the Sherragh Vane* and *The Schoolmaster* made up from sheets of the first edition of *The Doctor*
(3) *The Manx Witch and other Poems.* 1889	Macmillan and Co.		
(4) *Old John and other Poems.* 2nd edition, 1893	Macmillan and Co.	1st edition, 1889	*Old John* contained most of T. E. Brown's shorter poems. (Prefatory note by T. E. B.: 'The thanks of the author are due to the proprietors of the *National Observer* for permission to print some poems which have already appeared in the columns of that journal')

ABBREVIATIONS IN THE FOLLOWING PAGES

M.W. = *Manx Witch and other Poems*, edition 1889.

F.Y. = *Fo'c's'le Yarns and other Poems*, edition 1889.

Dr = *The Doctor and other Poems*, edition 1891.

O.J. = *Old John and other Poems*, edition 1893.

C.P. = *Collected Poems*, edition 1900.

SEPARATE ITEMS IN T. E. B.'S COLLECTED POEMS

Title	Date of composition	Previous publication
I. ASPECTS AND CHARACTERS		
Braddan Vicarage[1]	—	*O. J.*
Old John[2]	Clifton, 1880	*I.O.M. Times.* Reprinted in pamphlet form, and *O. J.*
Chalse a Killey[3]	Port Erin, 1875	*I.O.M. Times.* Reprinted as flysheet and *O. J.*
In the Coach[4]	Ramsey, Sept. 1891	*O. J.*
Mater Dolorosa[5]	—	*O. J.*

1 The home of T. E. Brown from 1832 till the beginning of 1847. Autobiographical.

2 John McCulloch came to the Isle of Man as a youth of eighteen and married a Scotchwoman living in the Island. As manservant to T. E. Brown's father he lived in a cottage almost opposite the old vicarage. After his wife's death his daughter and her husband lived with him. When Brown's father died little Maggie mentioned in the poem was about five years old. They continued to live with Old John till 1848 so that Brown's visit to his old friend must have taken place during his King William's days. Old John died in 1854 aged 77. 'Maggie', who became the wife of a builder, spent most of her life in Douglas, but after her husband's death removed to Ramsey. She is said to be still living (1929).

'The intrepid maid' mentioned in the poem was Margaret Wilson, a girl of eighteen, drowned in Solway Firth for her covenanter faith.

3 A wandering *character* crazed on Popery and religion. The *Life of Archdeacon Philpot* contains a reference to Chalse's visits to Wm. Drury when curate of Andreas. Drury's people lived at Union Mills. On one occasion when Chalse called there Miss Drury disguised herself as an Irish girl and came into the kitchen where Chalse was sitting. Chalse thought she really was Irish and therefore a Roman Catholic. 'I'll have her out!' shouted Chalse, and it was with difficulty he was prevented from putting her out. It was T. E. B. who asked Chalse to preach a sermon to himself and the painters at the Dhoor chapel on the Andreas Road about a mile and a half from Ramsey. Chalse is buried at Lezayre under the name of Charles Gill, an English form of his name.

4 A series of humorous yarns supposed to be heard in the coach which formerly plied between Douglas and Ramsey. *Jus' the Shy* is based on a yarn told to the poet by a Port Erin fisherman.

5 This was number 7 of a series, the first 6 of which are unpublished.

Title	Date of composition	Previous publication
The Christening[1]	Dec. 1878	*M.W.*
Peggy's Wedding[2]	1878	*National Observer* and *M.W.*
The Peel Lifeboat[3]	May 5, 1891	*O.J.*
Catherine Kinrade[4]	June 1878	*I.O.M. Times* and *O.J.*
A Dialogue between Hom-Beg and Ballure's River[5]	Probably after retirement to Ramsey	*C.P.*
Gob-ny-Ushtey[6]	—	*O.J.*
Failand. Portbury[7]	—	*C.P.*
The Dhoon[8]	Sept. 1875	*C.P.*
Wastwater to Scawfell	Nov. 1868	*C.P.*
The Well	March 1870	*C.P.*
Roman Women[9]	Ramsey, 1895	*New Review*, Aug. 1895

1 The speaker is the father, Edward Creer.

2 In a note to the editor the author quoted Swift as his model.

3 Written on T. E. B.'s birthday. Story of the wreck of a Norwegian ship in October 1889. The lifeboat crew battled all day against the wind over the six-mile course to the ship. The injured sailor afterwards died. Charlie Cain's widow a few years ago received a letter from the mate of the wrecked *St George*, saying he was now reaching the end of his life's voyage and expected soon to meet his old shipmates in heaven. The figure-head of the *St George* is now outside the Peel Lifeboat House.

Brown's attitude to conventional ideas of 'saint' and 'sinner'. In a letter to John MacMeikin in 1879 he vigorously rebutted the charge of being unorthodox.

4 In response to a request from John MacMeikin, the poet sent him a copy of *Catherine Kinrade* written from memory, with an accompanying letter dated October 1889. He had not preserved the copy printed in the *Isle of Man Times*. (These letters are preserved in the Manx Museum Library.)

5 Ballure lies at the foot of a mountain, and forms the southern end of Ramsey, where the poet lived in retirement.

6 A waterfall between Easy Cushlin and Creggan Mooar in the S.W. of the Island.

7 Places near Clifton.

8 A picturesque waterfall about two miles north of Laxey.

9 Based on the poet's observations during his visit to Rome at Christmas, 1879. Selwyn Simpson gives the first poem of the series, which is omitted in the *Collected Poems*.

Title	Date of composition	Previous publication
In Memoriam	—	*O. J.*
Song	—	*O. J.*
Dunoon	—	*O. J.*
The Laugh	—	*O. J.*
'Ne sit Ancillæ' [1]	—	*O. J.*
Whitehaven Harbour	—	*O. J.*
Ibant Obscuræ	St Bees, Aug. 1868	*O. J.*
St Bees Head [2]	St Bees, Aug. 1868	*O. J.*
An Oxford Idyll	Oxford, 1875	*O. J.*
Scarlett Rocks [3]	Aug. 1883	*O. J.*
Lime Street [4]	Aug. 1883	*O. J.*
Hotwells	Clifton, June 1868	*O. J.*
To K. H.	—	*O. J.*
Clifton [5]	Clifton, 1869	*O. J.*
In a Fives'-court	Probably 1875	*National Observer*, April 1892
The Lily-Pool [6]	Clifton, June 1868	*O. J.*
'Not willing to stay'	St Bees, Aug. 1868	*O. J.*
Ecclesiastes [7]	Clifton, May 9, 1869 (after chapel)	*O. J.*
Indwelling	—	*O. J.*
Salve!	—	*O. J.*
In Memoriam Paul Bridson [8]	Probably 1876	*O. J.*
In Memoriam A. F.	—	*O. J.*
Canticle	—	*O. J.*
White Foxglove	Ramsey, 1895	*New Review*, Oct. 1895
Octaves [9]	Ramsey, 1895	*New Review*, July 1896

1 Title suggested by Horace, *Odes* II, 4.
2 Original title, *Cliff Studies*.
3 On western horn of Castletown Bay.
4 A Liverpool thoroughfare and railway station.
5 The original MS had 'my feet for six long weary years have trod', which on publication was altered to 'thrice nine weary years'.
6 MS presented to H. G. Dakyns.
7 Note on original MS: 'This happened yesterday'.
8 The poet had visited Braddan in February 1876.
9 Suggested by a weaver and his wife living at Ballaglass.

Title	Date of composition	Previous publication
Poets and Poets	St Bees, Aug. 1868	*O. J.*
Opifex	Clifton, Oct. 1868	*O. J.*
In Memoriam J. Mac-meikin[1]	—	*O. J.*
'God is Love'[2]	Clifton, April 1883	*O. J.*
The Intercepted Salute	Coniston, July 1869	*O. J.*
Μεταβολή	—	*O. J.*
Jessie	Clifton, July 1868	*O. J.*
A Wish	—	*O. J.*
Dante and Ariosto	—	*O. J.*
Boccaccio[3]	Clifton, Feb. 1881	*O. J.*
To E. M. O.[4]	—	*O. J.*
Carol	—	*O. J.*
M. T. W.[5]	Clifton, 1886	*O. J.*
The Organist in Heaven[6]	Clifton, May 5, 1878, T. E. B.'s birthday	*O. J.*
To E. M. O.[7]	May 6, 1878	*O. J.*
A Sermon at Clevedon	—	*C.P.*
A Fable	—	*C.P.*
The Pessimist	—	*C.P.*
On the sinking of the 'Victoria'	Ramsey, July 1893	*National Observer,* July 1893
Χρῖσμα[8]	March 1874	

1 John MacMeikin was a Castletown banker. The poet had correspondence with him regarding Chalse-a-Killey and Catherine Kinrade. Brown's original letters are kept in the Manx Museum.

2 Derbyhaven, the scene of this incident, is the hamlet where T. E. Brown lived when Vice-Principal of King William's College.

3 Originally called *Sonetto*.

4 E. M. Oakeley, one of his colleagues at Clifton, January 1867 to April 1886.

5 Reference to Maurice Temple Wilson, son of the Principal of Clifton, who died this year, aged ten.

6 MS given to E. M. Oakeley. Original title, *Wesley in Heaven*. The reference is to Dr S. S. Wesley the composer.

7 See above.

8 To his godson—Henry Graham Dakyns, Junr.

Title	Date of composition	Previous publication
II. NARRATIVE		
Prologue Spes Altera[1]	June 1896	*I.O.M. Times,* Sept. 5, 1896
To sing a song shall please my Countrymen[2]		
Betsy Lee[3]	—	(a) *I.O.M. Times;* (b) *Macmillan's Magazine,* Apr. and May 1873; (c) *Every Saturday,* XIV, 527, 559–585; (d) Volume form 1873 and *F.Y.*
Christmas Rose[4]	—	*I.O.M. Times* and *F.Y.*
Captain Tom and Captain Hugh[5]	—	*I.O.M. Times* and *F.Y.*
Tommy Big-Eyes[6]	—	*I.O.M. Times.* Reprint from newspaper type 1888 and *F.Y.*
Dear Countrymen[7]		
The Doctor[8]	—	*I.O.M. Times.* Reprint from newspaper type 1876 and *Dr*

1 Prologue to whole series of *Fo'c's'le Yarns.*

2 Prefatory poem to *Fo'c's'le Yarns,* 1881 edition.

3 Brown's earliest Manx yarn. The scene is laid at Derbyhaven, where the poet lived as Vice-Principal of King William's College.

4 A story of a girl rescued from a shipwreck as an infant; who when she grows up resists all would-be lovers and dies tragically in a thunderstorm.

5 Story of rival Castletown skippers, illustrating Manx love of exaggeration. Powerful description of drowning scene.

6 Romance of the Curraghs picturing the emotions of a musician; a girl's unconsciousness of her evil surroundings; and the exposure of a hypocrite.

7 Prefatory poem to *The Doctor and other Poems,* 1887.

8 Generally considered Brown's masterpiece. Tale of a fine character driven to intemperance through frustrated love, but finally redeemed through the devotion of his daughter by the worthless woman he married.

Title	Date of composition	Previous publication
Kitty of the Sherragh Vane[1]	—	*Dr*
The Schoolmasters[2]	—	*Dr*
First comes Tom Baynes[3]	Clifton, April 1889	
The Manx Witch[4]	—	*M.W.*
Job the White[5]	MS dated 'Ramsey 1895' but written in 1894	*New Review*, 1897
The Indiaman[6]	—	*M.W.*
Mary Quayle (the Curate's story)[7]	—	*M.W.*
Bella Gorry (the Paᵹon's story)[8]	—	*M.W.*
Envoy to Fo'c's'le Yarns: 'Go Back!'	Feb. 1881	*C. P.*
III. LYRICAL		
Clevedon Verses[9]	July 1878	*O. J.*
Lynton Verses[10]		*O. J.*
(a) *Symphony*	Lynton, April 1877	
(b) *Lynton to Porlock*	July 1877	*O. J.*

1 Romance of a mountain farmer's daughter.

2 A humorously exaggerated picture of old-time elementary teaching. 'Danny Bewilder' never taught at the Lhen School—which exists to-day—but belonged to the Dhoon. Brown often used the place-name Lhen fictitiously. The New Testament was the reading-book used in such schools a hundred years ago.

3 Preface to *The Manx Witch and other Poems*, introducing the several narrators of the yarns included in the volume.

4 Story of a Laxey miner's courtship, introducing Manx folklore, customs and superstitions.

5 A philosophical sequel to *The Manx Witch*.

6 Founded on the narrative of a sailor, the prototype of Tom Baynes.

7 Story of a noble fisherman's self-abnegation. Scene laid in North of Island.

8 The incarnation of mother love. Scene laid in the Ayres on N.-W. coast of the Island.

9 References to his lad Braddan who died in 1876. In a letter written in November 1894 Brown said: 'Clevedon sums up our life even more than Clifton'.

10 To H. G. Dakyns and M. Dakyns.

Written on his way home from Lynton to Bristol.

Title	Date of composition	Previous publication
The Empty Cup[1]	St Bees, Aug. 1868	*O. J.*
Pain	—	*O. J.*
The Pitcher	Clifton, July 1868	*O. J.*
Song	—	*O. J.*
Veris et Favoni	—	*O. J.*
In Gremio	—	*O. J.*
Exile	—	*O. J.*
Climbing	—	*O. J.*
Risus Dei	—	*O. J.*
Dartmoor (Sunset at Chagford).[2] *Homo loquitur. Respondet* Δημιουργός	—	*C. P.*
The Prayers	—	*O. J.*
Ποιημάτιον[3]	Clifton Chapel, March 1874	*C. P.*
Juventa Perennis	—	*C. P.*
Vespers	May 1878	*C. P.*
I bended unto me a Bough of May	May 1878	*C. P.*
Is it Amavi or is it Amo?	—	*C. P.*
A fragment. You bird	—	*C. P.*
To W. E. Henley[4]	—	*C. P.*
When Love meets Love	May 1878	*C. P.*
Between our folding lips	May 1878	*C. P.*
Ex Ore Infantis[5]	Dec. 1894	*C. P.*
O God to Thee I Yield[6]	—	*C. P.*
To G. Trustrum[7]	Ramsey, Dec. 1895	*C. P.*
An Autumn Trinket	Oct. 1870	*C. P.*

1 A cliff study.

2 Personal. The MS contains no revisions.

3 Inscribed: 'for J. P.' John Percival, Principal of Clifton and afterwards Bishop of Hereford. Under the title *Top o' th' Hill* this poem appeared in the *Church Monthly* shortly after the author's death.

4 See Crypt School. The reference is to the death of Henley's child—a little girl.

5 MS presented to Miss Graves of Peel who had told the author the story of a dying child. Brown said he 'liked setting these little jewels'.

6 See Aber Stations.

7 On receiving a Christmas Card from George Trustrum, landlord of a hotel at Port Erin. A copy appears in S. T. Irwin's *Letters*.

Title	Date of composition	Previous publication
Reconciliation	July 1875	*C. P.*
Sad! Sad!	—	*C. P.*
In a Fair Garden	—	*O. J.*
The Schooner	Clifton, Oct. 1868	*C. P.*
Euroclydon	—	*O. J.*
Disguises[1]	Oct. 1875	*O. J.*
My Garden	July 1875	*O. J.*
Land, Ho!	July 1875	*O. J.*
Praesto	July 1875	*O. J.*
Evensong	July 1875	*O. J.*
Aber Stations (Stations of the Cross)[2]	Llanfairfechan, April 1879	*O. J.*
A Morning Walk	Clifton, Nov. 1868	*O. J.*
Epistola ad Dakyns[3]	Clifton, Dec. 1869	*O. J.*
Nature and Art	—	*O. J.*
Life	July 1878	*O. J.*
Alma Mater[4]	Clifton, Nov. 1868	*O. J.*
Triton Esuriens	St Bees, Aug. 1868	*O. J.*
Israel and Hellas	Clifton, June 1868	*O. J.*
Dreams	Clifton, June 1868	*O. J.*
Preparation	—	*O. J.*
Planting	—	*O. J.*
Obviam	—	*O. J.*
Specula	—	*O. J.*
Social Science[5]	—	*O. J.*
At the Play[6]	—	*O. J.*

1 An allegory expressing the poet's belief that in the crises of life there is ever in reserve a divine invisible hand to send the lifeline.

2 Aber is a Station of the Cross just beyond Llanfairfechan. The waterfall is about three-quarters of a mile from the station, with steep rocks and precipices. When Braddan accompanied his father in 1875 he imagined the rock would yield to his pressure. Revisiting it the following year the poet saw a dead lamb at the bottom of the precipice and was afterwards haunted by the feeling of the presence of Braddan, who had died in 1876. The MS was given to a friend and inscribed, 'God bless *your* lambs'.

3 Dakyns, who survived Brown by about fifteen years, was probably his closest friend.

4 Original title, *Mother Earth*.

5 Semi-humorous refusal to alter his views at the request of his friends.

6 Written for S. T. Irwin, with accompanying Latin translation, not published.

POEMS BY T. E. BROWN

(Not included in the *Collected Poems*)

These may be seen in the Manx Museum Library to which I am indebted for extracts of Brown Bibliography prepared by the Librarian in 1929

Date	Description	Publication
	Early Poems	Selwyn G. Simpson's *Appreciation of T. E. Brown* (Walter Scott Publishing Co. 1906)
1878	Series of humorous verses	*I.O.M. Times*
1879	*To Pazon Gill*	*I.O.M. Times*
Aug. 1893	*Cupid's Garden*	Dialect poem quoted in a lecture
Oct. 1893	*Nell Corso*	*National Observer*
Mar. 1894	*Jack Sartfell and his wife Nan*	Sung by Brown at one of his Peel lectures
1894	*The Gel of Ballasallaw* (words and music)	—
Sept. 1895	Three Manx Songs	*Ramsey Courier*
Nov. 1895	*To Sir West Ridgway* (Sonnet)	*I.O.M. Times*
Dec. 1895	T. E. B. to H. G. D.	MS
Jan. 1896	*Ramsey Isle of Man to Haslemere Surrey*	*I.O.M. Examiner*
July 1896	*In Memoriam Alexander Wood* (Sonnet)	*New Review*
Mar. 1897	*Festinatio Veres*	*New Review*
May 1897	*Laxey Lacrymans*	*I.O.M. Times*
Aug. 1897	Song for *Mheillea* tableau at Ramsey	Written for Miss Paton, Ramsey
Sept. 1897	St Matthew's Bazaar—Dialect verses	Handbook, Brown and Son (*I.O.M. Times*)

PROSE COMPOSITIONS BY T. E. BROWN

A Collection of these may be seen in the Manx Museum Library

Date	Title	Publication
May 1868	'Christ Church Servitors in 1852. By one of them'	*Macmillan's Magazine*
1869	'Manx Proverbs and Sayings'	*Manx Miscellany*
1877	'How to spend 7 days in the Isle of Man' and 'How to use the Manx Railways'	Brown's (*I.O.M. Times*) *Guide to the Isle of Man*
1885	*Castletown*	A 2 pp. pamphlet. Brown and Son (*I.O.M. Times*)
1890	Review of Hall Caine's *Bondman*	*Scots Observer*
Oct. 1892	Article on Pusey	*National Observer*
Nov. and Dec. 1892	'Rights of Way in the Isle of Man'	*Ramsey Courier*
Nov. 1892	Review of A. W. Moore's *Diocesan History*	*Ramsey Courier*
1893	Series of articles on 'Manx Character'	*Ramsey Courier*
—	Review of Walpole's *Land of Home Rule*	*National Observer*
Nov. 1894	Review of Hall Caine's *Manxman*	*Contemporary Review*, vol. LXIV, p. 643 (proof sheets preserved in the Manx Museum Library)
Dec. 1894	'Shakespeare at Maughold'	*Ramsey Courier*
Mar. 1895	'Lobster Salad'	*London Home Monthly*
Apr. 1895	'Hig ee foast' (She will come yet)—A tale of Glen Meay	*I.O.M. Times*
—	*Baron Knapp* (tale of Douglas in the 'Forties)	Serial in *Ramsey Courier*
—	'Old Manx Captains' (three articles)	*The Tourist*
Sept. 1895	'Robert Burton'—A causerie	*New Review*
—	Preface to Ryding's *Manx Tales*	John Heywood, Manchester
—	*Appeal for St Matthew's New Church*	Pamphlet. Brown and Son (*I.O.M. Times*)

Date	Title	Publication
Feb. 29, 1896	'Poosey dy moghey as poosey dy mennick' (Marry early and marry often)	*I.O.M. Examiner* (MS preserved in Manx Museum Library)
Apr. 1896	'Spenser'—A causerie	*New Review*
—	'Sir Philip Sidney'	*New Review*
May 1896	'Ben Jonson'—A causerie	*New Review*
1896	Preface to A. W. Moore's *Manx Ballads and Music*	
1897	*Manx Idioms* (summary of lecture at Castletown)	Pamphlet
—	'St Matthew's Old and New'	Brown and Son (*I.O.M. Times*)

During the poet's retirement he contributed a number of articles to the *Ramsey Church Magazine* edited by Rev. E. C. Paton. These included a series entitled *Manxiana*, which dealt with the lives of noted Manx clergymen of the nineteenth century and gave extracts from letters of Manx celebrities of the eighteenth century.

A collection of Brown's Letters, with an introductory memoir, edited by S. T. Irwin, one of his colleagues at Clifton, was published in 2 vols. by Constable and Co. in 1900. An index was added in the third edition.

The Manx Museum Library is now in possession of many of the originals of this collection, but they represent only a part of the Brown letters known to exist.

Sir Hall Caine, alone, has more than the total in the Museum: but, though they are full of vivacity and humour, the novelist considers them too intimate and confidential to permit of exhibition or publication.

T. E. BROWN MANUSCRIPTS IN THE MANX MUSEUM LIBRARY

Red Manuscript Note Book dated August the 2nd, 1855.

Contents.

    (1) Political Songs of Old England.
    (2) Sir Walter Raleigh and the old English Navigators.
    (3) How to be Healthy, Wealthy and Wise.
    (4) How to read History.
    (5) The History of Music.
    (6) Christianity and the Fine Arts.

Black Manuscript Note Book.

Contents.

    (1) Rev. Mr Gill (a fragment).
    (2) Pusey.
    (3) Bunyan.
          Sir Philip Sidney—A Causerie.
          English Literature—Race and Climate.
          Euphiusus.
          Chaucer.
          The Pagan Renaissance (a typed lecture).
          Notes of lecture on Clarendon Museum.

Letters.

    (1) To his mother and sister Margaret (Mrs Williamson).
    (2) To John MacMeikin.
    (3) To Hanby Hay (American poet).
    (4) Various.

    Note. Letters written between Sept. 1895 and April 1897 to Mr Charles Roeder, archaeologist and geologist, are deposited in Manchester Reference Library, and were reprinted in *Mannin*, No. 9.

List of proposed articles for *National Observer* on Sidney, Spenser, Ben Jonson, Burton's *Melancholy*, Sir Thomas Browne, Raleigh, Hook, ChristChurch, *The Manxman*.

ARTICLES ON T. E. BROWN AND HIS WORKS

These may be seen in the Manx Museum Library

Date	Publication and Title	Author
May 1892	*National Observer*: series 'Modern Men'. (Photo. Dean)	
Apr. 1893	*The Speaker*. 'A Morning with a Book'	A. T. Q.-C.
Aug. 1895	*Household News* (Philadelphia). 'Isle of Man and some Manxmen'	Hanby Hay
May 1897	*Bookman*. (Photo. Cowen)	William Canton
Nov. 1897	*The Times*. Obituary notice	Ven. J. M. Wilson
Nov. 1897	*Oxford Magazine*	Bishop Percival
Nov. 1897	*Academy*	
Nov. 1897	*New Review*. 'In Memoriam T. E. B.'	W. E. Henley
Nov. 1897	*I.O.M. Times*. 'In Memoriam.' (Wired from Paris)	Hall Caine
Nov. 1897	*I.O.M. Times*. 'His last days'	Rev. J. Williamson
Nov. 1897	*I.O.M. Times*. 'Tom Brown.' (Sonnet)	Edward Priestland
Nov. 1897	*I.O.M. Times*. 'T. E. Brown.' (Tribute of an old pupil)	Horatio F. Brown
Nov. 1897	*Spectator*. 'T. E. B.'s Dialect Poetry'	
Nov. 1897	*Glasgow Herald*	Dr Stewart Cowen
Dec. 1897	*New Review*	William Storr
Jan. 1898	*I.O.M. Times*. Poem 'Victory'	Hanby Hay
Apr. 1898	*Quarterly Review*	
Apr. 1898	*Fortnightly Review*, vol. LXXIV	S. Hughes-Games
Apr. 1898	*Pall Mall Magazine*, vol. XXII	W. E. Henley
Apr. 1898	*Macmillan's Magazine*, vol. LXXXII	J. C. Tarver
Apr. 1898	*Monthly Review*, vol. I, p. 152	A. T. Q.-C.
Aug. 1901	*Temple Bar*	J. R. Mozley
Dec. 1901	*Great Thoughts*. (Photo. Cowen)	J. Joughin

Date	Publication and Title	Author
1908	*Good Words*, vol. LIX (Photo. Cowen)	William Canton
1914	*Poetry Review*. 'The Homer of the Isle of Man'	Thomas Sharpe
1920	*Nineteenth Century*. 'T. E. B. Manxman, Scholar-Poet'	J. C. Tarver
Oct. 1929	*Church Quarterly Review*	Rev. Dr E. J. Martin

BOOKS AND PAMPHLETS CONTAINING REFERENCES TO T. E. BROWN

Dictionary of National Biography.

Encyclopaedia Britannica. (T. E. B. by A. T. Q.-C.)

Through a Cornish Window. (A. T. Q.-C.)

Little Manx Nation, p. 48. (Hall Caine)

Miles's Poets of the 19th Century.

Manx Worthies. (A. W. Moore)

T. E. Brown the Manx Poet. (Selwyn G. Simpson, with preface by J. M. Wilson)

Clifton Memories. (J. R. Mozley)

The Diary of a Fag. (Sir F. G. Newbolt)

Clifton 40 years ago. (Sir F. G. Newbolt)

T. E. Brown, Patriot. (William Cubbon)

T. E. B. and others. (W. R. H. C.)

The Lure of the West Country. (W. R. H. C.)

Redland Chapel. (H. J. Wilkins, D.D.)

The Great Manx Poet. (H. J. Wilkins, D.D.)

Bristol Times and Mirror, May 1st, 1928.

Speeches at unveiling of T. E. Brown bust at Douglas Town Hall, July, 1909.

Canon Wilson's speech at unveiling of memorial tablet at Ramsey, June, 1914.

Addresses at Annual Meetings of World Manx Association since 1914.

T. E. BROWN MEMORIALS AT REDLANDS AND CLIFTON

A marble cross erected over Brown's grave has the following inscriptions:

'Rev. Thomas Edward Brown, died Oct. 29th, 1897, aged 67;
Amelia (his wife), died July 3rd, 1887, aged 57;
Braddan (his child), died April 21st, 1876, aged 7.'

On a panel:

'Thomas Birkett Brown, son of above, died July 5th, 1919.'

MEMORIALS AT CLIFTON COLLEGE

Portrait of T. E. Brown by Sir William Richmond, in the College Library.

A bell inscribed with T. E. Brown's name.

A stained glass window in the College Chapel is dedicated

to the memory of Braddan Brown, Nat. 1869, Ob. 1876
and Maurice Temple Wilson, Nat. 1876, Ob. 1886.

INDEX

INDEX

For EU product safety concerns, contact us at Calle de José Abascal, 56–1°,
28003 Madrid, Spain or eugpsr@cambridge.org.

www.ingramcontent.com/pod-product-compliance
Ingram Content Group UK Ltd.
Pitfield, Milton Keynes, MK11 3LW, UK
UKHW030903150625
459647UK00021B/2651